Christianity:
The Faith That
Makes Sense

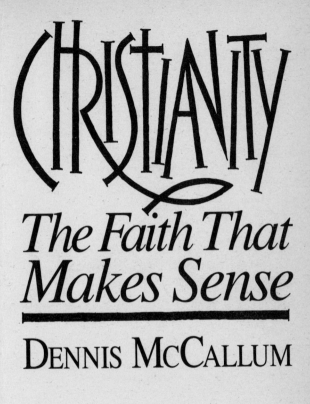

CHRISTIANITY

The Faith That Makes Sense

DENNIS McCALLUM

LIVING BOOKS®
Tyndale House Publishers, Inc.
Wheaton, Illinois

Visit Tyndale's exciting Web site at www.tyndale.com

Living Books is a registered trademark of Tyndale House
Publishers, Inc.

ISBN 0-8423-0535-1

Printed in the United States of America

02   01   00   99   98   97
8   7   6   5   4   3   2   1

CONTENTS

Introduction

Nothing in this life is as exciting as the experience of meeting and knowing the God of the universe. Even those who have not had this experience must admit that, if it were possible, it would be the greatest thing imaginable. This book is intended to help people meet God. Some of us have doubts or pains that make us feel unable to place our trust in God as we now understand him. If you are open to the idea of knowing God, this book should help you overcome those barriers.

In my experience as a Bible teacher and lecturer I am often asked for the name of a book with some good reasons for believing in Christianity. There are many such books. However, some of my favorite reasons or arguments are hard to find. Also, some of the most popular arguments in use today are problematic, either because they employ selective use of evidence or because the conclusion is not as clear as the authors claim. Others demand a leap of blind faith.

Christians need an explanation for our beliefs that will stand up to modern criticism. Such an argument may not build an inescapable case (and, in fact, this can never be done with any view), but it can give a good foundation upon which to base both our faith and confidence. Some of the best reasons for belief in Christ are to be found in the Bible's own defense of itself. We will examine these bases for faith as they are argued in the Bible.

I hope that the following pages will provide a few defenses for Christianity, while remaining readable even to non-Christians and those who are not familiar with the Bible. In fact, it is the non-Christian with whom I am most eager to speak. There are many good arguments not found in this book. However, these arguments are good examples of what can be expected, along with a short response to some of the main objections to Christianity. Finally, we offer some suggestions for those who decide to investigate further, including those who want to seek a personal relationship with God through Christ.

My thanks go to the following friends who

have selflessly spent many hours editing and advising me in this project: Keith McCallum, Steve Houser, Jeff Gordon, Maran Brainard, Kevin Abrams, John Circle, Jim Nye, Fred Alger, Jim Leffel, Brian Gardner, Chris Lang, and my wife, Holly.

ONE
The Worst Party Ever

Imagine yourself being ushered into a large party room with numerous booths, each offering a different activity or product. You can do anything you want at this party. Thousands of people are busily moving from one booth to another engaging in various pursuits. Some booths are offering art and music lessons. One popular booth offers assorted sexual experiences. Another booth offers drug experiences. A very large booth offers exercises which, when completed, will enhance one's body. Another offers tasks that entitle the participants to be rich. Yet another booth is a laboratory for scientific research.

However, there is a problem. You can only stay at the party for a short time because, unfortunately, you have already been infected with a virus that will kill you in three hours, if not sooner. The same is true for everyone else at the party. Everyone will die within three hours of the time they entered the party.

To make matters worse, as you visit the various booths, looking for something to do, you see several people suddenly collapse in sickness and die shortly afterward. Guards carry them out to be buried. Before long you begin to notice you are feeling sick. The onset of the illness begins to worry you and robs you of all the fun of the party. You realize your time at the party has a finite limit, and there is nothing anyone can do about it. The party becomes increasingly difficult to enjoy.

Have you ever considered that this situation might be exactly what we face? Our span of time might be seventy years instead of three hours, but the effect would be the same. Compressing the time span into three hours only makes it easier to understand the problem.

Back to the party. Perhaps as you consider the tragic nature of your situation, you realize you don't want to engage in any trivial activity. So you go to the laboratory. After two hours of intensive work, you discover a medication that will enable everyone to live for three hours *and five minutes!* Yet you find yourself wondering whether you have really contributed anything worthwhile.

Once again, we see that if life is only three hours long, it renders everything we do unimportant and meaningless in the end. The same would be true for a personal love relationship you might initiate during the party. You would no sooner begin to enjoy the relationship than either you or the other person would fall dead, rendering the whole thing meaningless.

As you try to consider what to do next, you might even find yourself wondering whether or not to simply end your life immediately and have done with it.

This is the way life looks to those who don't believe in an afterlife. According to such a view, we could do anything we want in this life, but the moment we die, everything would be canceled out. We would have no memory of what we did or who we were. We would simply cease to exist. Even those still alive would not really be affected because they die too. Eventually, the whole universe would fizzle out, and everyone would die. How, then, can anything matter in the long run?

On the other hand, perhaps there is such a thing as an afterlife. This would affect our lives no less.

Back at the party, as you are wandering from

booth to booth, you hear someone trying to get your attention. Looking over, you see a man standing by the corner of a booth near the wall, gesturing for you to come over. You walk over and ask him what he wants. He says, "We've found a door here that the others don't even know about! You can walk out of this door and receive a cure that enables you to live forever! You can return to the party and enjoy it without the symptoms you've been experiencing."

Obviously, such a claim would be suspicious. It might be a trick. It certainly seems too good to be true. Yet, while caution would be reasonable, probably you would be inclined to go over and see what he has. If you're like many people, you would want to see evidence that this door is authentic. Under the circumstances, it would be unthinkable to walk away without even investigating. The possibility that the door might offer a cure would be too important to ignore.

So it is with the possibility of eternal life. Although the analogy of the party is not perfect, it does demonstrate that the incentives for looking into the possibility of eternal life are very strong.

At the same time, we will see that exploring the possibility of an afterlife means we are really exploring God. This is because the existence of an afterlife implies that people are more than physical matter. For instance, a human body weighs the same amount one minute after death as it did one minute before death. What evidence is there that anything leaves the body at the time of death? Clearly, if anything did leave, it's not measurable, as physical matter would be. A soul or spirit that could survive physical death must be nonmaterial.

Many today believe we can account for the development of our physical bodies through the process of organic evolution. But how could a purely physical and material process such as organic evolution ever produce a nonmaterial soul or spirit that would survive death? Such a transition would mean that matter spontaneously gave rise to nonmatter, that the natural gave rise to the supernatural, that something came out of nothing. This is nonsense! If we have a spirit, it must originate from a spiritual source, such as God. This is why, when we contemplate the nature of an afterlife, we are really contemplating God.

THE DOOR TO HEALTH

At the party, you open the door the man has shown you. On the other side is God—personal, loving, and all-powerful. He welcomes you and immediately grants you the promised eternal life. This book is about such a door. A door to health in this life, and a door to life after death.

Jesus Christ said, "I am the door; if anyone enters through Me, he shall be saved" (John 10:9, NASB). Jesus was aware of the human dilemma illustrated in the description of the party above. He gave a similar illustration in the parable of the rich fool (Luke 12:16-21). This man labored all his life to build up a vast treasure, but he had ignored the temporal nature of life. When God confronted the rich man, he said, "You fool! This very night your life will be demanded from you. Then who will get what you have prepared for yourself?" (verse 20). In other words, what good is your accumulation of treasures when you will suddenly die and lose the ability to use or enjoy those treasures?

Equally foolish was the hedonistic alternative the man chose after his money-making was done. He said, "Take life easy; eat, drink and be merry" (verse 19). While eating, drinking, and being merry are not wrong, the problem lies in what he *failed* to do. The temporary stimulation of his body was a poor substitute for the real love that could have filled his life with significance while it also prepared him for the next life. He could have eaten, drunk, and been merry at the same time he applied himself to understanding his Creator.

Instead of giving in to hedonism, the man should have paid more attention to the question of what happens after his short time of treasure-gathering was over. Jesus sharply criticized the mentality that loses itself in the present and ignores what is coming in the not-too-distant future. Of the rich fool he said, "So is the man who lays up treasure for himself, and is not rich toward God" (verse 21, NASB).

It would have been so easy, according to Christ, for the rich fool to avoid this futile end. Jesus claimed: "I am the resurrection and the life. He who believes in me will live, even though he dies; and whoever lives and believes in me will never die" (John 11:25-26).

Here again Jesus claims he is a door—a way out of futility. This way out, if it exists, would make everything we do significant and meaningful because our actions in this life would carry over to the next.

Let's suppose for a moment that a Creator God does exist, and that we are the products of special creation. This would not necessarily mean there is no such thing as evolution. It would mean, however, that God may have intervened at certain points in the development of the world, particularly at the point where humans were created. Such an intervention would account for the features we see in ourselves that lead us to think we are persons, not just random formations of molecules.

It would be great news if such a personal Creator God existed, and if we were created in his image, as the Bible claims. It would mean that our life might not be without purpose. It would mean that relationships we enter into might have eternal significance. It would mean that contributions we make to the human condition in this life may not just prolong the misery, but might be truly important.

But is there a way to tell if such a God exists? Further, if he does exist, what might he be like, and what might he want from us? Can Jesus Christ be relied upon to reveal the truth about God? We would have to be very careful to avoid simple wishful thinking in this area. It would be all too easy to choose to believe something simply because we wanted to believe it.

Many people believe wishful thinking is exactly what faith is all about, but we will see this is not the case. On the contrary, we will see more than enough satisfying evidence to support personal faith in Jesus Christ.

TWO
Faith or Reason?

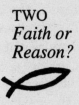

Before we can begin looking into the question
of the authenticity of Jesus Christ and the Bible,
we should establish some ground rules for the
discussion. If we can agree on the following
principles, we will have a basis for communication. Even if we don't agree on all the principles, at least you, the reader, will understand
what the basis of this discussion is.

GROUND RULE 1: REASON WORKS

When determining whether to believe the Bible,
we can use reason as well as experience. We can
rely on conclusions we reach through reason,
even though some things must be experienced to
be understood. In the Bible, Paul told his readers
there is such a thing as "love that surpasses
knowledge" (Ephesians 3:19). This suggests we

can have mystical or experiential knowledge. On the other hand, he also said, "We persuade men," which shows that he saw a place for reason when discussing spiritual things (2 Corinthians 5:11). According to the biblical worldview, we are dealing with a combination of reason and experience.

But mystical knowledge is also *compatible with* rational truth. Your sense that a painting is beautiful might not be something you could defend rationally, but neither is it incompatible with reason. On the other hand, the idea that one God may exist for me and a different one for Hindus is not compatible with reason. To accept different realities for different people, we would have to take leave of reason, or we would have to argue that this truth is beyond human reason. In either case, reason has lost its value in determining truth.

In our postmodern culture, we speak of people living different realities. But this expression refers to the idea that people's *experience* of reality is different depending on their cultural upbringing. It does not mean that for people raised in China the sun doesn't exist, or that there is no gravity in Africa. There is a reality inside our minds—the reality of our experience. But we also must consider a reality outside and independent of what we think. We hear challenges often today to the idea that so-called linear reasoning can tell us anything certain about the world. But all these challenges are based on the same thing: linear reasoning!

No one has ever escaped the bounds of rationality, and no one needs to do so. We will be considering biblical faith: neither reason without experience nor mysticism without reason, but a combination of both. It's the same in so many areas of life. I have reason to believe my wife exists—not only because I could measure her with scientific instruments, but also because of my personal experience of her. Both of these lines of evidence are valid. Neither contradicts the other.

If we agree reason can tell us something about reality, we must be prepared to reject contradictory things.[1]

GROUND RULE 2: LET'S BE FAIR

If we are fair, we will take a neutral posture when determining what to believe. This means the burden of evidence does not lie exclusively with either the one who believes in the God of the Bible, or atheists or other religionists. For instance, if we flipped a coin and covered it with a book, it would be either heads or tails. How can the one who believes it's heads argue that the other person has the responsibility to prove it's tails?

Suppose you were looking for a jar of jelly you lost. You'd start by looking in the cupboard

that seems most likely to contain it. You don't
know for sure whether it's there, and you don't
need to know before looking. Likewise, with
our worldview, we only have to discern that one
alternative is more plausible than the others to
have a real basis for moving in that direction.

GROUND RULE 3: NO INESCAPABLE PROOF

There is no inescapable "mathematical" proof
that any worldview is true. This means there
will be no such inescapable proof for Christianity either. Even if we claim we believe in nothing at all, we have decided to take a position
that has no inescapable proof. Such a decision
depends on faith—faith that nothing merits personal belief. Every point of view requires faith
in some first principles. That's why, if we think
about it, we don't need absolute proof for Christianity. Instead, the case for Christianity
depends on *inductive reasoning,* which means
that we consider evidence and weigh the prob-
able truth by a given position.

GROUND RULE 4: EXPERIENCE MUST BE ADDED TO REASON

Eventually it will be necessary to turn to God personally and experience the new life promised by
Jesus Christ (John 1:12). If we think about the illustration of the misplaced jelly, it's easy to see why

experience should be combined with reason. You stand in front of the cupboard realizing this is the most likely place to find the jelly. You don't know for sure, but you realize you have sufficient reason to open the cupboard and look. Once you open it, you become sure—either that the jelly is there or that it isn't—based on your experience.

The Christian position is that God exists and that he is concerned about you. This concern is so deep that God has gone out of his way to demonstrate the truth about himself to anyone who will listen. By studying this demonstration, you can reach a place where you have good and sufficient reason for taking a "step of faith," where you embrace the claims of God on the basis of reasonable evidence, hoping for further confirmation, including personal experience. There is no reason to discount the validity of any experience with God that might result from such a step of faith. As the love of God fills your heart, you may become certain that you have indeed met God personally. Such experiences are different from a religious experience with no rational foundation of any kind.

GROUND RULE 5: MORE THAN ONE LINE OF EVIDENCE

For some of us, any single line of evidence may not be sufficient to establish the "good and sufficient reason" we need in order to accept or reject the Christian position. We may need to consider several lines of evidence before we make such a decision.

We will be considering the case for biblical Christianity. You may think other religious systems have reasonable bases essentially the same as those for Christianity. Actually, this is not true. As we shall see, religious traditions often make little or no effort to give objective evidence for their teachings.

But before we even consider the evidence for biblical Christianity, we need to define what this message is. Many diverse doctrines can be found under the name "Christianity" today, and many have no backing other than the say-so of religious leaders. We must agree on what Christianity is before looking at the evidence.

NOTES

1. The doctrine of the Trinity is not irrational. A God who is "Three in *person* and one in *essence*" (as the creed says) is not self-contradictory.

THREE
The Core of Christian Teaching

The heart of the Christian message can be summarized in the word *grace*. Grace means a gift. God wants us to understand through the Bible that he has something he wants to give us.

THE NEED FOR GRACE

The Bible teaches that the human race has fallen from the state God intended for it. This fall fundamentally altered our moral nature (Genesis 3; Romans 5:12-21). Therefore, the current state of affairs is essentially abnormal and twisted. God created the world not only in perfection but also with real freedom. Now that humans use their freedom to turn away from God's leadership, the world is spinning somewhat out of control. Not only humans but the world itself is in a severely damaged and

15

distorted condition as a result of the free choice of humankind (Romans 8:20).

We will discuss the objections to this position later. The main point for now is that, as the Bible describes it, the central problem in our world is the evil in the human race resulting from our separation from God. The Bible places the blame for the present situation squarely on humankind, maintaining that God is guilty of nothing more than creating freedom.

The Bible teaches that all humans are guilty of evil much of the time (Romans 3:9-18; Mark 10:18). Note that this guilt is not referring to guilt *feelings*. Instead, we are being told that, regardless of what we feel, we are guilty of moral offenses against the character of God. Even when we do something not specifically evil, we may fail to act under the leadership of God, and therefore such works fall short of God's standard of perfection (Romans 14:23). This is because doing the right thing is not enough. God wants us to do the right thing *and* to do it for the right reasons (1 Corinthians 4:5).

The Bible goes further, arguing that people are helpless in their wrongful way of life. Although we had freedom at one time, we have lost the freedom to live without sin and are now helpless in our selfishness (John 6:44, 65; Romans 5:6, 8, 10).

We might say the Bible has a radically negative view of humankind on the moral level. At the same time, the Bible argues for the high value of human life and the beauty of human creativity because people were created in the image of God (James 3:9). Although people have fallen from their original state, this image of God is still evident—just sadly twisted.

When we see the Bible allowing no exceptions to the depravity of human nature, either for race, sex, or social class, we realize this message is unusual. The idea of the fallen nature of humanity, so central to the Bible's message, sharply diverges from what we like to think about ourselves. Yet we should view this negative part of the Bible's message along with the positive part—the dynamic liberty possible through God's grace.

When you think about it, there *must* be something wrong with our race and with our world! How can anyone look at disfigured newborns, endless war and cruelty, and the sheer devastation we wreak on our environment and argue that nothing is amiss? We will be discussing the problem of evil in detail later, but for now, we can hopefully agree that people in our world

have a negative twist at the same time they have
a unique beauty.

GOD'S RESPONSE TO HUMAN EVIL

We can appreciate the Christian concept of
grace by comparing the biblical message to the
message of other religions. Most religions realize there is something wrong with humankind.
This realization probably accounts for people's
universal sense that they need to practice some
form of self-punishment in order to avoid divine
judgment. Most religions hold that people must
work at following various religious laws in
order to earn the favor of God. The more wrongdoing in someone's life, the more moral credits
he must earn.

Most religions teach that it's up to the worshiper to do what is acceptable to the deity in
order to attain salvation. He then grades people
according to their performance in the area of
religious laws and ritual. Some Christian
churches teach this as well. However, the teaching is alien to the New Testament and therefore
is not a part of biblical Christianity.

The notion that God requires the observance
of ritual and other religious regulations in order
to avoid divine judgment raises serious problems. For one thing, it makes God seem harsh
and unwelcoming. We seem to have a God who

is holding up a hoop and saying, "Here, let's see you jump through this." If we do so, he says, "Do it again," and eventually, "Now keep doing it for the rest of your life." After the worshiper's death, God decides whether reward or punishment will be handed out, and to what degree.[1]

In many cases, the laws handed down have no apparent beneficial effect on the worshiper (for instance, reciting the same prayer several times a day facing Mecca, or reciting the same prayer ten times in a row). It seems like the act is more for the benefit of the deity than for the worshiper. But this is a problem also. What benefit does God need? If he is the Creator of everything, what does he gain from having his creatures go through repetitive motions? Here some rather disturbing motives suggest themselves.

In fact, according to this prevailing view, God seems to be quite callous and unwelcoming. He seems to grudgingly hand out blessing and acceptance only if we earn them through hard work. All who fail do so are ignored or destroyed. He doesn't seem eager to see many people receive blessing. If he were eager, wouldn't he dispense with the hoop? Wouldn't he seek to do something about the vast majority who are not observing the religious disciplines? There is almost a hint of sadism here, or at least a definite reluctance to accept people.

Biblical Christianity disagrees more sharply in this area than in any other. According to Jesus, "Even the Son of Man did not come to be served, but to serve, and to give his life as a ransom for many" (Mark 10:45).

According to the New Testament, Christ's incarnation solves the problem between God and people caused by evil. Even though people are responsible for every evil thought and deed, God does not want to see us undergo punishment for our sin. Therefore, Jesus came to die, suffering the judgment of God in our place, so that we would not have to bear that judgment. In other words, God underwent his own judgment so that we could receive salvation as a free gift. God now wants us to accept this gift, even though it may feel humiliating to accept something for free.

Many passages in the New Testament stress that God offers the gift of salvation through Christ freely to anyone who wants it. In Ephesians Paul explained it this way: "For it is by grace you have been saved, through faith—and this not from yourselves, it is the gift of God—not by works, so that no one can boast" (Ephesians 2:8-9).

This passage squarely denies that God has a hoop of religious laws through which we must jump. Instead, it affirms that we can do nothing except receive this gift of faith—faith that the death and resurrection of Christ will put us right with God.

WHY SO MUCH HASSLE?

We may wonder at this point, Why would God go through all the trouble of the Incarnation and the Cross? If he wants to accept people, why not simply ignore the fact that they misbehave and accept everyone? When we look deeper into the nature of God, we will see that such a simple answer won't work.

God's character is said to be just (Romans 3:26). In other words, God cannot overlook the present rebellion on earth and the actions that flow from it. God's justice requires a fair and impartial punishment for all sin. To understand this, suppose our evil acts resulted in the same consequences as our good acts. This would suggest that God makes no distinction between good and evil. The difference between good and evil would be nothing but words if God reacted the same way to both. This would be no less alarming than the nasty, rejecting God pictured earlier in the religious law model. An amoral God would be capable of anything, and certainly would provide no answers to our dilemma. Also, if God sees atrocities on earth but assigns no blame to the human race, it implies that he feels something or someone other than humanity is to blame. This raises several problems as we shall see later. The Bible teaches that since we have free will, we alone are responsible for our rejection of God's leadership, and we must give an account of our life.

At the same time, the Bible teaches that this need to judge sin is unpleasant to God because of his great love for us (2 Peter 3:9; 1 Timothy 2:4; Ezekiel 18:23; 33:11; Lamentations 3:32-33). God is in a dilemma because he loves us; yet, because he is just, punishment is required.

THE RADICAL SOLUTION

The Bible also explains how God solved the dilemma. It was a difficult problem that required a radical solution. The solution he came up with is called *atonement*. This means that sin must still be paid for, either by ourselves or by someone else. But who else could pay for our sins? Obviously, one man can't bear the consequences for another because he has his own sins to account for. Even if there were a perfect man with no sins of his own to worry about, he could only pay the price for one other man. That would be fair—one sinless person substituting for one guilty person.

But if the moral problem was to be solved for all people, someone had to take all the punishment deserved by all people upon himself. This would require an infinite person. This is why God decided to come himself in the person of Christ and undergo his own sentence on behalf of his wayward creatures.[2] The Bible explains this solution in Romans: He did this so that "He might be just and the justifier of the one who has faith in Jesus" (Romans 3:26, NASB).

To understand the phrase "just and the justifier," we can turn to a simple illustration.

THE FAIR JUDGE'S SON

The story is told of a judge who lived in a small town with his family. He was the fairest judge anyone could remember and had faithfully served the community for many years. One night the judge's son went out, got drunk, and raped and killed a girl in town. He was caught and brought to trial before his own father.

The people in the town wondered what the judge would do. Since the judge had always been impartial, they thought he would give his son the electric chair. On the other hand, he really loved the boy. Would he sacrifice his love for the sake of justice? Or would he sacrifice justice for the sake of love and unfairly let his son go free? Indeed, exactly this kind of conflict of interest would lead us to assign a different judge to this case—a luxury God doesn't have.

When the trial began, the courtroom was full. As the evidence was presented, it became clear the boy was guilty. Finally the judge swung his gavel and said, "Guilty as charged! And the sentence is to be execution in the electric chair!"

A gasp went though the courtroom. Certainly, what the judge did was fair, but how could he do that to his own son? But at that moment, the judge arose and went over to sit in the witness chair. Then he said, "But I will serve the sentence for him!"

As the judge was led away to his death, the boy walked out a free man!

Before we feel too bad about the guilty boy getting away with murder in this story, we should remember that the boy represents you and me. According to the Bible, we are under a sentence of death, "for all have sinned and fall short of the glory of God" (Romans 3:23). And, "The wages of sin is death, but the gift of God is eternal life in Christ Jesus our Lord" (Romans 6:23).

At the Cross God became both the *just* and the *justifier*. He showed that he was *just* because he did not simply ignore sin but administered the full and fair punishment. Yet he was the *justifier* because he had given all men the option of escaping punishment at his own expense.

The fact that God was willing to go to this

length to solve a problem that was not of his own making is an amazing fact to anyone who examines it. At the Cross God demonstrated his love in an incontestable way. He now offers you this forgiveness as a gift—the gift of grace that stands as the center post of the biblical message.

> But when the kindness and love of God our Savior appeared, he saved us, not because of righteous things we had done, but because of his mercy. He saved us . . . through Jesus Christ our Savior, so that, having been justified by his grace, we might become heirs having the hope of eternal life. (Titus 3:4-7)

WHAT ABOUT THE LAWS?

One might wonder why God gave us moral laws in the Bible (like the Ten Commandments) if salvation is a free gift. This is answered in Romans also:

> Therefore no one will be declared righteous in [God's] sight by observing the law; rather, through the law we become conscious of sin. But now a righteousness from God, apart from law, has been made known. (Romans 3:20-21)

In other words, the religious laws in the Bible are different from those of other religions because they are not given in order to secure salvation. Instead, this passage says the law can only make us "conscious of sin." Like a mirror that shows us dirt on our face, the law shows us we fall short of the moral standards of God. The mirror cannot remove the dirt; it only shows that it is there. Consider, for example, the law described in Deuteronomy 6:5: "Love the Lord your God with all your heart and with all your soul and with all your strength." This law, if taken seriously, even allowing for a figure of speech, cannot be kept. We have all surely broken it already and will break it many times in the future as well. Such laws express perfect moral ideals. God never expected that we would keep them. He gave them to show us that we fall short of what we should be doing. This is what Paul meant in the passage cited above: "Through the law we become conscious of sin." Once we realize we fall short of God's standards, the stage is set for us to turn away from self-effort and receive the free gift of forgiveness in Jesus Christ.

The Old Testament law shows us our need for Christ. However, once we accept his grace, we are no longer under law: "For sin shall not be your master, because you are not under law, but under grace" (Romans 6:14).

> Before this faith came, we were held prisoners by the law, locked up until faith should be revealed. So the law was put in charge to lead us to Christ that we might be justified by faith. Now that faith has come, we are no longer under the supervision of the law. You are all sons of God through faith in Christ Jesus. (Galatians 3:23-26)

How different this is from other religious systems! Of course, the fact that we are not under law does not imply that there is no right and wrong for a Christian. It does mean, however, that doing good cannot save a person and doing wrong will not condemn a person if that person has received the grace of Christ.

People still have to personally receive the gift that God offers: "Yet to all who received him, to those who believed in his name, he gave the right to become children of God—children born not of natural descent, nor of human decision or a husband's will, but born of God" (John 1:12-13).

Notice this passage indicates there is no privileged race, class, or sex in Christianity. This truth is confirmed in Romans: "This righteousness from God comes through faith in Jesus Christ to all who believe. There is no difference, for all have sinned" (Romans 3:22-23).

This is why Paul can summarize the Christian message this way: "For we maintain that a man is justified by faith apart from observing the law" (Romans 3:28).[3]

CONCLUSION

In most religious thinking, we have a severe God who for some reason holds up a hoop for people to jump through. In the Bible, we see a picture of a God who has done all the jumping himself at great personal expense.

If I made up a new religion, I might put myself in God's place and conclude that if I were God, if I had supreme power, I would certainly get mine first! I might find it implausible to forgive someone who is really bad without asking for some penance first. I might find myself willing to consider forgiving someone, but not if he keeps doing the same thing again and again.

Yet in the Bible we are confronted with someone different from ourselves. God is prepared to offer forgiveness so complete that it removes the question of sin from the discussion. Then we become free to relate to God on the basis of a love relationship instead of legal performance.

This relationship is available without charge to anyone who will turn to God in faith and act on what John 1:12 promises: "To all who received him, to those who believed in his name, he gave the right to become children of God."

To *receive* means that you consciously tell God that you accept his terms for a relationship: that you need to be forgiven, that Christ's death is the only thing that can pay for your sins, and that you want his Spirit to come into you. Some of us may think that faith means we have no doubts. This is not true. When Jesus asked one man why he doubted, the man pleaded, "I do believe; help me overcome my unbelief!" (Mark 9:24).

This, then, is the heart of biblical Christianity. If there is compelling evidence behind the Christian message, it would be great news: a doorway leading to freedom and life! We are ready now to turn to that evidence.

NOTES

1. It would not be difficult to document that virtually all religions holding for a personal afterlife teach this notion, although it would take up too much space for our purposes. Even in religions that teach an impersonal afterlife, Karmic

law is the key to Moksha or Nirvana. For now, it is sufficient to see that Islam, Judaism, and Catholicism (according to most historical formulations) believe worshipers are
responsible to perform good works and obey religious laws
to a standard that will make them acceptable to God.

Thus the Talmud teaches, "At the time of a man's depar-
ture from this world, all his actions are detailed before
him. . . . He agrees, and is then ordered to sign the record.
He also admits the justice of the verdict and declares,
'Rightly hast Thou judged me'" (*Taanith,* 2a). Rabbi
Zakkai laments at the time of his death, "If [God] is angry
with me, His wrath can be unending; if He imprisons me,
it can be forever; if He slays me, my death will be eternal;
and I can neither appease Him with words nor bribe Him
with money. Moreover, two paths now lie before me, one
leading to Paradise and the other to Gehinnom [hell], and
I know not which I am destined to take. Should I then not
weep?" (*Berachoth,* 28b). (Both available in translation in
R. Alexander Feinsilver, *The Talmud for Today* [New York:
St. Martin's Press, 1980], pp. 214–216.)

In the case of Islam, "If any do deeds of righteousness,
be they male or female and have faith, they will enter
heaven" (*The Koran,* Sura 4:124). Again, "There will be
there all that the souls could desire, all that the eyes could
delight in . . . such will be the garden of which ye are made
heirs for your (good) deeds (in life)" (Sura 43:72; see also
3:15; 4:57; 4:69; 4:124; 5:122; 7:43; 9:20; 9:72; 37:40).
There are six duties or pillars required in order to be saved:
(1) citing the creed (2) prayer five times per day (3) alms
giving (1/40 of one's income) (4) fasting during the holy
month (5) pilgrimage to Mecca unless prevented by war
or circumstances beyond control (6) holy war—the duty
to strive for the triumph of Islam over other religions. (Sir
Norman Anderson, *The World's Religions* [Grand Rapids,
Mich.: Eerdmans, 1976], p. 78.)

Roman Catholicism also teaches that good works are the

key for salvation, along with faith. "Justification is con-
ferred in baptism, the sacrament of faith," according to
the new Catechism. However, justification is no guarantee
of eternal life. "Since the initiative belongs to God in the
order of grace, *no one can merit the initial grace* of forgiveness and justification, at the beginning of conversion.
Moved by the Holy Spirit and by charity, *we can then merit*
for ourselves and for others the graces needed for our sanc-
tification, for the increase of grace and charity, and for the
attainment of eternal life" [emphasis original] *(Catechism
of the Catholic Church* [Liguori, Mo.: Liguori Publications,
1994], pp. 482–483). Thus, one needs a combination of
baptism, faith, and good works, or "merits" to make it to
heaven. Although many Catholics today may not hold this
view of salvation, it is still the predominant view, and it is
still the only view officially sanctioned by the Vatican.
Indeed, many Jews and Muslims may deviate from these
views as well. The point here is that these religious worldviews originally taught that keeping religious law is the
key to eternal life.

2. The amount of judgment due for human sin is infinite.
This is because God's character is infinite. We may wonder
how Christ could receive an infinite amount of punishment
in the finite time he was on the cross. The answer is that
infinite judgment could be expressed either as finite wrath
for an infinite time (hell), or as infinite wrath for a finite
time. Only with his divine, infinite nature was Christ able
to accept infinite punishment in a moment of time. This is
one reason why the deity of Christ is an essential point in
Christian teaching.

3. We have based much of this discussion on Romans 3
because the gospel of Christianity is clearly and fully
explained there. However, it would be a mistake to think
that this is an isolated teaching. The same points are
repeated in many other passages. Those desiring more

study on the subject might consider these passages to begin with: Luke 18:9-14; John 3:16; 5:24; 6:29; 15:1-8; Acts 16:30-31; Romans 5:20; 7:1–8:1; 1 Corinthians 6:9-11; 2 Corinthians 3:6-11; 5:19-21; Galatians 2:16; 3:24-25; Ephesians 4:32 (note completed action, "forgave"); Colossians 2:13; Hebrews 10:10-17; Jeremiah 31:31-34; Ezekiel 36:25-27.

FOUR
Does the God of the Bible Exist?

Before turning to the evidence that applies
exclusively to Christianity, we should take a
few minutes and consider whether the whole
notion of God's existence deserves our attention.
Although most people believe God exists, many
of us do not know why our belief is reasonable.
This chapter describes some of the lines of
reason used by philosophers and scientists to
explain why believing in God is intellectually
defensible. You could skip this chapter if you
are one who already believes in a personal God.

When looking at arguments based on the
nature of the world around us, we have to realize these arguments may not specifically point
to Christianity but to the worldview under-
lying Christianity—*theism.* To understand the
difference between theism and other possible

worldviews, I have included a chart (see pages 36–37) comparing the major views in the world today. If we can determine that theism (the belief in an infinite, personal God) is credible, we can then look at options within theism to determine whether one of them stands out as particularly convincing.

With these definitions in view, we can turn to a few selected lines of reason that suggest theism is perhaps the most credible of all possible worldviews.

THE ARGUMENT FROM DESIGN

The presence of design in nature implies that there must be a Creator God. How do we think the complex world in which we live came into being? Naturalists would argue that since energy is able to enter our world, and the building blocks were already present, chance collisions of molecules could produce life.

Theists answer that even though energy is free to enter the system of our world, there is no mechanism to explain how chaos could have produced order and complexity unless someone with purpose and intelligence caused it to do so. For instance, we could put some dynamite under a pile of bricks and blow it up. The system contains sufficient energy and the correct building blocks to build the Taj Mahal. But is it really plausible that blowing the bricks up would have this result? Even if we repeated the experiment millions of times over, it seems unlikely that it would ever result in the Taj Mahal or any other kind of building. Even if, after one of our blasts, we found one brick lying atop another, this would hardly prove that "if this much could happen, the rest could as well." Although the building blocks and energy are there, more is needed. The energy must be channeled in the very precise way required in order to produce a complex design.

Of course, the more complex the design, the more difficult it is to believe it happened by accident, and living organisms are much more complex than the Taj Mahal. Wouldn't it be more sensible to believe that someone acting with intelligence and purpose has arranged things this way?

Such an argument cannot prove a personal God exists. This is because some parts of the argument are subjective. For instance, what constitutes order? Isn't it our observation of an existing system and our labeling it as orderly that make this argument seem so plausible? This may be partially true, but in many of our minds there is adequate reason to consider things like living cells to be orderly, and orderly in a way that could never be explained

LET'S DEFINE OUR TERMS

It sometimes seems as if there are more philosophical and religious views than any normal person could ever learn about. Indeed, there are more than six thousand distinct religions in the world today. However, some are surprised to find that the world's religions and philosophies tend to break down into a few major categories. There are some views that don't exactly fit into one of these categories, but they are a tiny fraction of the whole. Here we have the four main ways of looking at reality.

	REALITY	MAN	TRUTH	VALUES
Naturalism Atheism; Agnosticism; Existentialism	The material universe is all that exists. Reality is "one-dimensional." There is no such thing as a soul or a spirit. Everything can be explained on the basis of natural law.	Man is the chance product of a biological process of evolution. Man is entirely material. The human species will one day pass out of existence.	Truth is usually understood as scientific proof. Only that which can be observed with the five senses is accepted as real or true.	No objective values or morals exist. Morals are individual preferences or socially useful behaviors. Even social morals are subject to evolution and change.
Pantheism Hinduism; Taoism; Buddhism; much New Age consciousness	Only the spiritual dimension exists. All else is illusion, *maya*. Spiritual reality, *Brahman*, is eternal, impersonal, and unknowable. It is possible to say that everything is a part of God, or that God is in everything and everyone.	Man is one with ultimate reality. Thus man is spiritual, eternal, and impersonal. Man's belief that he is an individual is illusion.	Truth is an experience of unity with "the oneness" of the universe. Truth is beyond all rational description. Rational thought as it is understood in the West cannot show us reality.	Because ultimate reality is impersonal, many pantheistic thinkers believe that there is no real distinction between good and evil. Instead, "unenlightened" behavior is that which fails to understand essential unity.
Theism Christianity; Islam; Judaism	An infinite, personal God exists. He created a finite, material world. Reality is both material and spiritual.	Humankind is the unique creation of God. People were created "in the image of God," which means that we are personal, eternal, spiritual, and biological.	Truth about God is known through revelation. Truth about the material world is gained via revelation and the five senses in conjunction with rational thought.	Moral values are the objective expression of an absolute moral being.

Spiritism and Polytheism Thousands of religions	The universe as we know it had a beginning and will have an end.	The world is populated by spirit beings who govern what goes on. Gods and demons are the real reason behind "natural" events. Material things are real, but they have spirits associated with them and, therefore, can be interpreted spiritually.	Man is a creation of the gods like the rest of the creatures on earth. Often, tribes or races have a special relationship with some gods who protect them and can punish them.	Truth about the natural world is discovered through the shaman figure who has visions telling him what the gods and demons are doing and how they feel.	Moral values take the form of taboos, which are things that irritate or anger various spirits. These taboos are different from the idea of "good and evil" because it is just as important to avoid irritating evil spirits as it is good ones.

(This chart was adapted from Jim Leffel, "Apologetics," an unpublished manuscript. See *Eerdmans' Handbook to the World's Religions* [Grand Rapids, Mich.: Eerdmans, 1982], also Denise and John Carmody, *Ways to the Center: An Introduction to World Religions*, [Belmont, Cal.; Wadsworth Publishing Co., 1984].)

by simple natural processes such as those put forward by naturalists so far. We need to remember that evolutionary principles, such as natural selection, do not apply here because the original formation of life would have been a nonorganic process.[1]

THE PRESUPPOSITIONAL ARGUMENT

When we combine the argument from design with another argument, the results are more convincing. In fact, as we shall see, the existence of a personal God becomes very difficult to deny. This argument is sometimes called the presuppositional argument for the existence of God. According to this argument, only the theistic worldview is consistent with its own *presuppositions*. We all have to begin somewhere in our thinking. These beginning views, or "first principles," are called presuppositions, because we presuppose that they are true. In order for any worldview to be believable, its conclusions must agree with its presuppositions. Otherwise the view contradicts itself and is irrational. For instance, if I claim I believe gravity has no effect on me, yet I always wear a parachute when flying, my life is inconsistent with my supposed beliefs.

An illustration may be the easiest way to understand this argument.[2] Suppose two men are riding in a railway coach, and, glancing from the window at one of the stops, they see numerous white stones scattered about on a small hillside near the train in a pattern resembling these letters: THE CANADIAN RAILWAY WELCOMES YOU TO CANADA. One man observes that it took a lot of work to arrange the stones in that pattern, but the other disagrees. The second man argues that there is no actual proof that any work was expended on the arrangement. After all, the stones are clearly present on other parts of the hill, and the fact that they are on a slope means they might roll down periodically. How can anyone prove the stones didn't just accidentally fall into this curious arrangement?

At this point, the first man may feel that the second man is being credulous and irrational, but, technically speaking, he has to admit there is no actual proof (from where they are sitting) that anyone arranged the rocks this way. Still, he feels his explanation is easier to believe than that of the second man, even though this judgment is somewhat subjective.

(So far, this is an argument from design as described above. Now observe a further step we can take in our thinking based on our presuppositions.)

A few minutes later, the second man suggests

they should get out at the station and exchange their U.S. currency for Canadian money.

"What makes you think we should do that?" asks the first man.

The second man answers, while pointing to the rocks on the hill, "Can't you read? It says we are entering Canada!"

Now the second man has demonstrated that he, too, believes the arrangement of the stones is no accident. The fact that he is drawing conclusions about the world based on the arrangement of the stones is inconsistent with his earlier claim that they had fallen into that pattern by accident. He wouldn't believe he was entering Canada unless he, too, thought the stones were placed in this arrangement by a purposeful being in order to communicate something.

APPLYING THE ANALOGY

In the same way, any time we use our reasoning ability to draw conclusions, and any time we look at patterns in the universe to discover truth (such as scientific laws), we are affirming by our actions that we already suppose there is a rational basis to the universe. Otherwise, why would we trust anything our rational minds tell us? Somehow, there must be a connection between our rationality and the structure of the universe. This could only be true if the universe has emerged from a rational source and is, in fact, reasonable in its very makeup. Today, postmodernists recognize this point and conclude that reason cannot be trusted.

Let's look at this another way. If everything was the result of chance and arose out of chaos (as atheists argue), then everything has been chemically determined. In other words, there is a cause-and-effect sequence in operation wherein each event has a given result. No outside influence (like the human mind) exists that is not also a part of this cause-and-effect chain. Why, then, would we think our own thought processes (themselves conditioned) could tell us anything about reality? Yet, if we go on to use our reason to interpret reality anyway, and we trust that our conclusions are telling us something about reality, we are like the skeptical man on the train mentioned earlier. We show by our actions that we believe in an orderly and rational basis to the universe.

Such confidence in reason is consistent with theism, not with naturalism. This reasonable and orderly basis to the universe, we argue, is none other than the reasoning and personal One who created all, and is himself the ground of all being.

The same argument applies in several other areas.

BELIEF IN FREEDOM

Most of us, including naturalists and post-modernists, often act and think in a way that implies we believe people are free in their choices. For instance, when we criticize rapists or tyrants for doing terrible things, we imply that they are able to freely choose what they do. Otherwise, why should we criticize them for doing what they must do in a deterministic system? The fact that we feel such outrage implies that we believe people are making free choices and that they are not marionettes on a string.

When we act as though we are free-choosing beings, rather than determined ones, we imply that there is a basis for freedom. But the idea that we are free is contradictory to the presuppositions of both naturalism and postmodernism. If we believe in freedom, it implies that we also must believe in a Creator God. Let's see why this is so.

When vinegar is poured over baking soda, it foams. This is a physical event leading to a chemical reaction. There is no freedom involved in such a reaction: the chemicals do precisely what the laws of nature prescribe under those circumstances. Likewise, according to the naturalistic worldview, our thought processes are nothing but chemical reactions in our neurons. Such reactions may be much more complicated, but they are also determined by the conditions and the laws of nature. If this is so, then, according to naturalists, what we perceive as free thinking is actually caused by the environment and is beyond our ability to control. But if our thought processes are not free, then any naturalist who tries to think or view others as though they were free is being inconsistent, like the skeptic on the train.[3]

Postmodern relativists also deny the basis for reason. They claim reason is nothing but a western European tradition used to cloak their real power agenda. Yet, when they argue this case, guess what they use? They use reason! They, like everyone else, cannot escape rationality, because rationality is part and parcel of the universe created by a rational God.

As theists, we argue, on the contrary, that the basis for real freedom is the eternally free and sovereignly choosing Creator God who has made us in his image. Our thoughts may involve chemical reactions, but we also have a mind, or a soul, which goes beyond the physical. Our will can govern our thoughts when we want it to. Our thoughts have meaning and importance because they are substantially free.

BELIEF IN MORALITY

We find the same sort of inconsistency when naturalists act as though there is such a thing as morality, even though they believe there is no Creator God. If we say there is such a thing as moral right and wrong, we are implying that there must be a universal and personal basis for morals. A minute of thought will show why this is so.

Is it morally wrong to sexually abuse three-year-olds? Is the rightness or wrongness of such an act purely a personal choice, or is there a universal moral standard at stake? If such a moral norm is universal and lies outside of the individual's decision, then such actions are wrong whether the perpetrator thinks so or not. However, such a universal moral norm must have a universal basis.

If the universe is nothing more than chemicals bumping into one another, as naturalists claim, such chance collisions cannot teach us that child abuse is wrong, or that human life matters. Quite the contrary! If we are purely matter, and are the result of material processes, then we are destined one day to perish as a race in the destruction of the present solar system. If this is so, what difference does it make how that matter is configured in the meantime? Whether our molecules take one form (a living person) or another (a decomposed body) would not be a moral issue. Without the moral authority of a personal Creator God, we are left with nothing but preference or expediency. We can speak about what we prefer or about what actions contribute to a given goal, but we cannot say anything is moral or immoral.

Likewise, postmodern relativists argue that people are the products of their cultures. They see all people trapped within the prison of their own language-paradigm. Yet, most postmodernists also push for universal acknowledgment that intolerance and oppression are morally wrong. If they were consistent with their own claimed views, they would never try to push their values onto others, as though they knew better. When postmodern thinkers argue for universal values, they betray their own philosophy.

In one area after another we will find that it is impossible to act consistently with worldviews that deny an infinite, personal, creator God. Such worldviews fail the test of internal consistency and should be rejected by honest thinkers. Instead, we should accept the fact that a personal moral and rational God has indeed created us and our world.

THE COSMOLOGICAL ARGUMENT FOR THE EXISTENCE OF GOD

Evidence is accumulating that the universe is finite. This finding leads to a powerful argument for the existence of a personal God.

Scientists are now virtually unanimous in saying that the universe is expanding. The movement of stars and galaxies away from each other can be measured. If all the galaxies are moving away from each other, this could not have gone on for an infinite period of time. If we reason backwards in time far enough, the stars and other matter in the universe must at one time have been together in one place. This is in fact what science teaches. At some point in time, the so-called big bang occurred, which sent the stars and galaxies hurtling out from one another as they still are today.

This means things have not always existed as they are now. What could have caused the big bang? Scientists have entertained the notion of an oscillating universe in an attempt to answer this question. According to this theory, if the universe contains enough mass, the gravitational pull of so much mass could eventually slow and even reverse the outward motion of the galaxies. Eventually, the universe would fall back into itself. The energy of so much matter crashing together might cause another big bang, and so forth, for eternity. In other words, the material universe is eternally oscillating in and out according to this view. However, many astronomers are now becoming convinced that there is not enough mass in the universe to arrest the

present momentum and accomplish this oscilla-
tion.[4]

This means either one of two things.

There may have only been this one big bang.
If so, there is no endless sequence of cause and
effect extending into the past. At least, there
would have to be some cause that we cannot imagine or describe based on our knowledge. Whether
this unimaginable cause is natural or is God seems
to be an even call. Belief in either would have to
rest on faith. It would be just as easy to believe
that cause and effect extend backward only a
finite distance and began in an uncaused cause,
the infinite, personal Creator God.

On the other hand, there could be matter in
the universe that we have not yet been able to
see or measure. This is the view accepted by
most naturalists today. But here is another leap
of faith. This is not belief in the evidence of the
senses, but faith in that which will fill the gap
and make this worldview tenable. Those holding such a view exert no less faith than theists.
In fact they exert far more faith —this is mystical or blind faith.

It should be clear from even this short survey
that theism is a worldview deserving attention.
Interestingly, all three of the major theistic religions in the world today trace their roots to one
source—the Bible. It is to this book that we turn

now to discover further compelling evidence that not only theism, but Christianity, deserves our fullest investigation.

NOTES

1. See a technical discussion of this question in J. P. Moreland, *Scaling the Secular City* (Grand Rapids, Mich.: Baker, 1987), pp. 43–75.

2. This illustration is adapted from a similar illustration by Richard Taylor, cited in John Hick, *Arguments for the Existence of God* (New York: Herder and Herder, 1971), pp. 23–24. See also J. P. Moreland, *Scaling the Secular City,* pp. 77–103.

3. Today naturalists try to argue that quantum physics has provided an explanation for how people can be free in a material universe. However, this advanced math has only demonstrated randomness, not freedom in the sense of free choice. Quantum physics cannot account for *intent* in human actions.

4. Robert Jastrow, *God and the Astronomers* (New York: Warner Books, 1978), pp. 108–109, 110–113. Note that Jastrow is a self-proclaimed agnostic scholar. See also Hugh Ross, *Cosmology Confronts the Creator* (Pasadena, Calif.: Reasons to Believe, 1987).

FIVE
God's Chosen Method of Self-Authentication

If you were God and you wanted to offer human-kind evidence that you existed and that people could reach you through a certain source, how would you do it? How would you distinguish your message from other false messages created by people for the purpose of manipulation? God wants to demonstrate the authenticity of his message, and we might call this *self-authentication*.

For God to authenticate himself, the evidence would have to be readily available to those interested. We would not expect it to be hidden or secret. If it is true that God faces spiritual opposition, it seems likely that such an opposition would try to counterfeit or discredit any evidence given. Therefore, God's means of self-authentication would have to be something unique—something that no one but God could do. It would have to stand up even under the closest scrutiny.

This kind of self-authentication would be quite difficult to obtain.

People usually think of a miracle—a supernatural event—as proof of the presence and working of God, but there are problems with this kind of verification. Suppose God had one of his servants heal someone. There would still be room for doubt. Perhaps the person wasn't really healed. Maybe the person didn't actually have the condition from which he was supposedly healed. Even if the person was healed, can't others do the same thing? It certainly would not be acceptable to have this kind of extraordinary healing reported secondhand. Such miracle stories are commonly heard from every imaginable religious group and usually are not true.

The same goes for other miracles. If a spokesperson for God rose up bodily into the air, we would have to point out that magicians float their subjects in the air and pass hoops over them all the time. I personally don't know how they do this, but I still don't believe it's a miracle. The same would go for burning bushes, walking on water, and other events that could be simple magician's tricks.

Suppose a column of fire appeared and a deep and powerful voice spoke out, "This is the Lord." This would certainly be impressive! However, from God's point of view, there would be problems. How often would he have to stage such an event? Would it be reasonable to think of God making such an appearance for every person on earth? If this were the case, it would require no faith at all to follow him. On the other hand, unless he did repeat it for everyone, we would be left with the secondhand report of others, which might not be convincing. After seeing such an event, I think I know what my first response would be: "Let's see that again!" Besides, even if we admit the event was a supernatural one, how would we know it came from the Creator God himself? Couldn't this event involve a supernatural entity other than the God of the Bible?

In fact, if we want to be critical, there are serious problems with most ways God could conceivably reveal himself. According to the Bible, God is not willing to override human free will in most cases, which rules out any coercion. For instance, Paul was struck blind on the road to Damascus, but this does not seem to be the norm. If God was prepared to overwhelm free will, there would be little reason to prolong the current phase of history. We will explain the reasons for this later. But for now let's just say the problem of self-authentication is not as easy as we might have thought at first.

THE BIBLICAL ALTERNATIVE

When we turn to the Bible, we find a surprising and satisfying response to the question of verification. The Old Testament book of Isaiah says God spoke through a prophet to indicate his displeasure with the way many Israelites were no longer worshiping him and were instead worshiping nature deities. To set himself apart from other so-called deities, God said: "I am the Lord; that is my name! I will not give my glory to another or my praise to idols. See, the former things have taken place, and new things I declare; before they spring into being I announce them to you" (Isaiah 42:8-9).

God says, "Before they spring into being I announce them." Only God can foretell the course of history. God challenged the idols Israel was worshiping to do the same:

> "Present your case," says the Lord. "Set forth your arguments," says Jacob's King. "Bring in your idols to tell us what is going to happen. Tell us what the former things were, so that we may consider them and know their final outcome. Or declare to us

the things to come, tell us what the future
holds, so we may know that you are gods.
Do something, whether good or bad, so that
we will be dismayed and filled with fear."
(Isaiah 41:21-23)

According to this passage, the litmus test of
real deity is the ability to know history before
it occurs. The ability to foretell events would
require one of two things: either the power to
cause history to unfold a certain way, or the
ability to step outside the constraints of time.
Either of these would indicate an omnipotent,
eternal being.

Of course, not all predictions of the future
would indicate deity. If the predictions were
general (something bad is going to happen
tomorrow) or commonplace (my wife will die
someday), they would prove nothing. On the
other hand, predicting the future course of history in a detailed way, spanning scores or hundreds of years, is something only God can do.
It therefore fits one of the key requirements we
saw earlier—the verifying act cannot be done
by anyone other than God.

In order to guarantee authenticity, the predictions must be set down in writing, and the
written material must be reliably dated before
the events described. Also, the predictions

should be detailed enough to make coincidence implausible.

The unique ability to tell the future, available only to God, is repeatedly stressed in this section of Isaiah. Examples of some of the statements in Isaiah follow:

> This is what the Lord says—Israel's King and Redeemer, the Lord Almighty: I am the first and I am the last; apart from me there is no God. Who then is like me? Let him proclaim it. Let him declare and lay out before me what has happened since I established my ancient people, and what is yet to come—yes, let him foretell what will come. Do not tremble, do not be afraid. Did I not proclaim this and foretell it long ago? You are my witnesses. Is there any God besides me? No, there is no other Rock; I know not one. (Isaiah 44:6-8)
>
> Ignorant are those who carry about idols of wood, who pray to gods that cannot save. Declare what is to be, present it—let them take counsel together. Who foretold this long ago, who declared it from the distant past? Was it not I, the Lord? And there is no God apart from me, a righteous God and a Savior; there is none but me. Turn to

me and be saved, all you ends of the earth;
for I am God, and there is no other. (Isaiah
45:20-22)

I am God, and there is no other; I am
God, and there is none like me. I make
known the end from the beginning, from
ancient times, what is still to come. I say:
My purpose will stand, and I will do all
that I please. (Isaiah 46:9-10)

I foretold the former things long ago,
my mouth announced them and I made
them known; then suddenly I acted, and
they came to pass. For I knew how stubborn
you were. . . . Therefore I told you these
things long ago; before they happened I
announced them to you so that you could
not say, "My idols did them; my wooden
image and metal god ordained them."
You have heard these things; look at
them all. Will you not admit them? From
now on I will tell you of new things, of
hidden things unknown to you . . . so you
cannot say, "Yes, I knew of them." (Isaiah
48:3-7)

Listen to me, O Jacob, Israel, whom I
have called: I am he; I am the first and I
am the last. . . . Come together, all of you,
and listen: Which of the idols has foretold
these things? (Isaiah 48:12, 14)

God returns to this area of verification again and again, stressing his uniqueness and the inability of other gods to do the same.

THE NEW TESTAMENT

Christ was also persistent in pointing to the issue of fulfilled predictive prophecy as the proof of his own authenticity. For instance, in Luke 24 Jesus pointed to the predictions of his actions in the Old Testament as the evidence that he was the savior of humankind. He said to his followers:

> "This is what I told you while I was still with you: Everything must be fulfilled that is written about me in the Law of Moses, the Prophets and the Psalms." Then he opened their minds so they could understand the Scriptures. He told them, "This is what is written: The Christ will suffer and rise from the dead on the third day, and repentance and forgiveness of sins will be preached in his name to all nations, beginning at Jerusalem. You are witnesses of these things." (Luke 24:44-48)

The other writers of the New Testament also argued that fulfilled predictions of Christ were the proof of his authenticity. Peter said: "This is how God fulfilled what he had foretold through all the prophets, saying that his Christ would suffer. . . . Indeed, all the prophets from Samuel on, as many as have spoken, have foretold these days" (Acts 3:18, 24).

Similarly, Paul argued that Christ should be trusted because he fulfilled prophecies: "As his custom was, Paul went into the synagogue, and on three Sabbath days he reasoned with them from the Scriptures, explaining and proving that the Christ had to suffer and rise from the dead. 'This Jesus I am proclaiming to you is the Christ,' he said" (Acts 17:2-3).

He summarized his approach in another passage: "For what I received I passed on to you as of first importance: that Christ died for our sins according to the Scriptures, that he was buried, that he was raised on the third day according to the Scriptures, and that he appeared to Peter, and then to the Twelve" (1 Corinthians 15:3-5).

The theme of verification through fulfilled prophecy is stressed in many other passages in the New Testament.[1]

Some predictions have little evidential value today. In a few cases, people disagree on how passages should be interpreted. In others, we cannot today independently verify the fulfillment.

On the other hand, many prophecies are easy

to interpret and can be independently verified, as we shall see. Other predictions are only now being fulfilled. In connection with one of these predictions, Jesus made a claim similar to that in Isaiah: "I have told you everything ahead of time" (Mark 13:23).

In saying this, Christ was exactly in line with what God holds forth in the Old Testament; that his authoritative nature is demonstrated by his ability to predict the future. The predictions coming true today, along with the ones that were fulfilled in the past, lead to a very convincing argument that the Bible is inspired. The Bible does predict the future course of history in a way that cannot be explained except as a product of divine inspiration.

STRONG ADVANTAGES

The idea of a self-autheticating written body of predictive material, which can be compared to subsequent history, has much to commend it. In the first place, it would not be necessary to have a live messenger present each time God authenticates himself. Of course, a human messenger would still need to originally record the predictive material. Others would have to copy the material. But this is still better than a live human agent speaking every time people are addressed. Given the unreliability of human preachers, and

the proven willingness of religious functionaries
to distort the truth for their own advantage or
wealth, God had good reason to use a written
medium to convey his Word.

God certified the authenticity of the written
predictions by seeing they were widely copied
and dispersed over a period of hundreds of
years. In order to do this, he selected a group
of people (the Jewish nation) who would take
it upon themselves to write and preserve this
Word. The Israelites did an excellent job for
God, carefully guarding the Bible scrolls over
a period of fifteen hundred years. We have
samples of the Old Testament Scriptures from
long before the time of Christ as well as afterward. They show that the Jews were extremely
careful in the transmission of their sacred text.

Some people question whether a written
source can possibly be trusted when people
make errors during copying and even deliberately distort the meaning. But we ought to ask
ourselves, If a written source is unreliable,
what kind of source *would* be reliable? An oral
source? An ecclesiastical office? No. Such
sources are even more likely to be distorted than
a written source. More important, scholars have
shown that with the numerous copies of the
Bible we have from different sources and peri-
ods, we can rest assured that the copy we have

today is very much the same as the copies dating back as far as hundreds of years before the time of Christ.[2]

With a written record, we won't have the experience described earlier upon seeing the power of God ("Let's see that again!"). We can return to the evidence as often and as long as we want to.

If God provided a list of hundreds of predictive statements about history, we could look at the predictions and compare them with the subsequent events described. If the predictions were precisely fulfilled, we would have some real evidence to consider.

Of course, there are others who claim to be able to foretell the future, even in our own day, but they can't do it. As God stated in Isaiah:

> I am the Lord, who has made all things . . .
> who foils the signs of false prophets and
> makes fools of diviners, who overthrows
> the learning of the wise and turns it into
> nonsense, who carries out the words of his
> servants and fulfills the predictions of his
> messengers. (Isaiah 44:24-26)

PHONY PREDICTIONS

Not all claimed predictions of the future are authentic. One source often believed to be predictive is Nostradamus. The following is an example of one of his predictions: "The senseless ire of the furious combat will cause steel to be flashed at the table by brothers: To part them death, wound, and curiously, The proud duel will come to harm France."

Surprisingly, this "prophecy," we are told, predicts the Camp David agreement between Israel and Egypt and the assassination of Anwar Sadat! The "table" refers to the bargaining table. The "proud duel" refers to international terrorism. The "harm" to France refers to the destabilization in the Near East since the death of Sadat.[3]

The critical reader will realize, first of all, that there is no context to guide the interpretation. These stanzas are routinely separated from one another and analyzed independently. In fact, there is not even syntax or grammar to indicate the meaning. Instead, the interpreter is attaching to the words any meaning he desires. The idea that a reference to brothers at a table in 1555 refers to these two men in 1978 is doubtful in the extreme. This is especially apparent when we are given no reason to follow such an interpretation.

Such unclear and inaccurate predictions were not acceptable in biblical times. People knew that if God said something would happen, it would happen! God would not be accurate only

20 percent of the time, or even 85 percent of the time. Only 100 percent accuracy would demonstrate the text is from God. This is why false prophecy was not a safe profession in ancient Israel. In Deuteronomy 18:20-22 God says:

> But a prophet who presumes to speak in my name anything I have not commanded him to say . . . must be put to death. You may say to yourselves, "How can we know when a message has not been spoken by the Lord?" If what a prophet proclaims in the name of the Lord does not take place or come true, that is a message the Lord has not spoken.

Because of the importance attached to this area of verification, God was tough on those who tried to masquerade as prophets. So-called prophets who made as many errors as modern prophets would have long since had their careers shortened!

As we turn to a few examples of fulfilled prophecy in the Bible, remember that God has given us this evidence because he loves us. He wants us to know he is there and that he is involved in the flow of history. He is not catering to our curiosity. He is calling us to realize

the implications of what we see and to turn to
him.

NOTES

1. There are far too many references to deal with here.
The following examples are not exhaustive: Matthew
1:22-23; 2:23; 5:17-18; 8:17; 12:17-21; 21:4-5; 26:56;
Luke 18:31-33; 24:25-27; John 1:45; 12:38; 13:18-19;
15:25; Acts 13:27-29; 26:22-23; 28:23; Romans 1:2-3;
1 Peter 1:10-12; Revelation 10:7.

2. The respected archaeologist W. F. Albright said, "We
may rest assured that the consonantal text of the Hebrew
Bible, though not infallible, has been preserved with an
accuracy perhaps unparalleled in any other Near Eastern literature." Cited in Gleason L. Archer, Jr., *A Survey of Old
Testament Introduction* (Chicago: Moody Press, 1974), p.
67. See Albright's articles "The Early Hebrew Manuscripts
and the Early Versions" and "Lower Criticism of the Old
Testament," pp. 3–67. Also see R. K. Harrison, "The
History of Hebrew Writing" and "The Old Testament Text,"
Introduction to the Old Testament (Grand Rapids, Mich.:
Eerdmans, 1969), pp. 201–243. For New Testament docu-
ment transmission, see F. F. Bruce, *The New Testament
Documents: Are They Reliable?* (Downers Grove, Ill.:
InterVarsity Press, 1960).

3. Jean-Charles de Fontbrune, *Nostradamus: Countdown to
Apocalypse* (New York: Holt, Rinehart and Winston,
1980), p. 52. This text is from Century II Q 34. Fortbrune
does not translate Nostradamus accurately into English.
See the correct translation of the text in Edgar Leoni, *Nostradamus and His Prophecies* (New York: Bell Publishing
Company, 1961), p. 171.

SIX
The Time of Christ's Coming Predicted

Literally scores of historical predictions in the Old Testament have come true. Those of particular interest to us are the predictions that foretell events or persons with accuracy and which could not have been faked or counterfeited. In the ancient book of Daniel we have one passage that is particularly impressive in its detail and accuracy. This is the prophecy of the "seventy sevens" in Daniel 9. The prediction is not discussed often for one simple reason: it is complicated. Yet it is precisely this fact that makes it remarkable. This is what the passage says:

> Seventy "sevens" are decreed for your people and your holy city to finish transgression, to put an end to sin, to atone for

wickedness, to bring in everlasting righteousness, to seal up vision and prophecy and to anoint the most holy. Know and understand this: From the issuing of the decree to restore and rebuild Jerusalem until the Anointed One, the ruler, comes, there will be seven "sevens," and sixty-two "sevens." It will be rebuilt with streets and a trench, but in times of trouble. After the sixty-two "sevens," the Anointed One will be cut off and will have nothing. The people of the ruler who will come will destroy the city and the sanctuary. The end will come like a flood: War will continue until the end, and desolations have been decreed. (Dan. 9:24-26)

In 539 B.C., we are told, a messenger from God came to Daniel with the vision above. The reference to "sevens" throughout the passage means sabbatical years, or seven-year units of time. This is clear from the earlier part of the chapter. In verse 24 it says that 490 years have been allowed by God for the Jewish people to, among other things, "bring in everlasting righteousness." Then the years are broken down into sections. In verse 25 he explained that: "From the issuing of the decree . . . until the Anointed One, the ruler . . . will be seven 'sevens' [49 years], and sixty-two 'sevens' [434 years]."[1]

This reference to the "Anointed One" (Hebrew, "Messiah") who will "put an end to sin," "atone for wickedness," and "bring in everlasting righteousness" is none other than the world Savior so often promised in the Old Testament.

This passage is amazing because it not only says such a savior will come, it also says *when* he will come!

Remember, the book of Daniel was written more than five hundred years before the time of Christ. As a matter of fact, we have segments of Daniel from the Dead Sea Scrolls and other sources that predate Christ.[2]

SO WHEN SHOULD HE COME?

What date, then, is being named for the coming of the world Savior? Amazingly, the prophecy begins in the fifth century B.C. and ends during the ministry of Jesus of Nazareth in the first half of the first century A.D.! The exact dates for the fulfillment can be worked out a couple of ways, but the outcome is never in doubt. Jesus Christ was predicted in a unique way centuries before he was born.

DATING DANIEL'S PROPHECY

To assign a date for the fulfillment of the seventy weeks prediction, we must determine the length of time predicted, the beginning point, and then the end.

The length of the interval. Observe again the wording of the prophecy:

> From the issuing of the decree . . . until the Anointed One, the ruler . . . will be seven 'sevens' [49 years], and sixty-two 'sevens' [434 years]. (9:25)

We see the "from . . . until" language here that specifies an interval of 49 plus 434 years, or a total of 483 years.

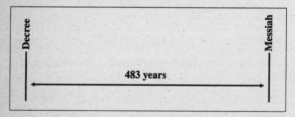

The beginning point. The beginning point is a "decree to rebuild Jerusalem," which stood in ruins at the time the book of Daniel was written. The issuing of this decree is recorded in Nehemiah 2:1-10, along with the exact date during the reign of Artaxerxes I.[3]

Any encyclopedia will show that Artaxerxes I was king of Persia from 465–424 B.C. Since the month of Nisan is in the spring, the actual date of this decree issued in the twentieth year of the king's reign was March/April 444 B.C."[4]

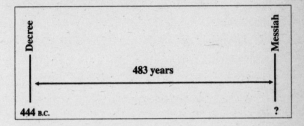

Historians don't question the fact that the Jews returned from captivity in Babylon and rebuilt Jerusalem at about this time, because it is well attested by independent sources. Remember, Nehemiah was also written hundreds of years before Christ, so it was not possible for him to "fix" the date.

The target date. The Hebrew year is 360 days (12 months of 30 days each), which is a total of 173,880 days. This is approximately 476 of our years. Since there is no such thing as a "0 year" in our calendar, we need to deduct one more year from the difference. Subtracting, we get $444 - 476 = -32 - 1 = -33$. The negative number indicates an A.D. date. In other words, when Hebrew lunar years are converted to modern solar years, the actual date indicated as the year that the Christ would come is A.D. 33! The more accurately the conversion is worked out, the more accurate the result.[5]

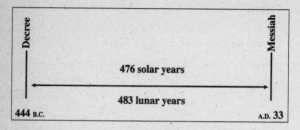

The best year for the fulfillment of Daniel's prophecy is A.D. 33. In the month of Nisan in A.D. 33, Jesus entered Jerusalem on a donkey's colt. This was the entry predicted by Zechariah:

> Rejoice greatly, O daughter of Zion! Shout, daughter of Jerusalem! See, your king comes to you, righteous and having salvation, gentle and riding on a donkey, on a colt, the foal of a donkey. (Zechariah 9:9)

WHAT ABOUT TRICKERY?

These two predictions form an interesting comparison. The one in Zechariah could have been faked by someone who wanted to pretend he was the Messiah by riding a donkey colt into Jerusalem while having his friends acclaim him as king. But Jesus could not have faked the prediction in Daniel, even if he had a motive for being the suffering Messiah.

With the advent of modern archaeology we are now able to determine the exact dates for events in the latter part of the Old Testament with far more accuracy than anyone could at the time of Christ. It would have been impossible for people at the time of Christ to determine the exact year this prophecy was fulfilled. They would not have known exactly how much time had passed since the decree was issued because accurate records had not been kept.[6] The people of Christ's time were aware that the prophecy of Daniel was due to be fulfilled soon, as witnessed by Josephus.[7] However, they were only aware that Messiah should come within a generation or so.

One other objection could be raised to this prediction. Namely, is it possible that the Gospel authors lied about the entire event? For several good reasons, the answer is no.

In the first place, the date of Christ's death is not directly stated in the Gospel records. Scholars base this date on other data in the Gospels that can be cross-checked with external sources. These data enable historians to determine that only April A.D. 30 or April A.D. 33 would meet all of the New Testament requirements. For instance, Pilate had to be in Galilee at the time of Christ's death. Also, Herod's temple had been under construction for 46 years at the beginning of Jesus' ministry (John 2:20). The latter date (A.D. 33) better accounts for the events mentioned in the Gospels.[8] Therefore, by correctly describing the situation in A.D. 33, the Gospel authors indirectly identified the correct circumstances surrounding the fulfillment of this prediction.

This means that for the authors of the Gospels to fake this passage, they not only would need to know the date they were faking, but they also would have to know what criteria modern scholars would use to fix a date for the event! Besides, if they wanted to fake a date, wouldn't they simply name that date in the usual way?[9]

The Gospel authors had no accurate calendar information on which to base a faked record, so how could they have been this accurate? In other words, we can't account for the accuracy of the prediction by claiming that the Gospel authors lied, because they would not have been able to lie this accurately!

Finally, even without any Gospel records, we would be able to determine that the essential facts in the prediction came true. We know from the ancient Roman historian Tacitus and the ancient Jewish historian Josephus that a religious leader named Jesus, founder of the Christian sect, was crucified by Pontius Pilate in Judea.[10] These secular sources had nothing to gain by referring to Christ. They refer to him because their sources indicated that his life was a historical fact.

Even without the statements these witnesses made about Jesus, we would know Jesus must have lived at about this time. This is because the Christian movement appeared by the middle of the first century with some force. Such a movement would have required some years of development, which points to the existence of a founder (Christ) sometime shortly before or after A.D. 30. We can narrow the date further by realizing that Pilate would have been in a position to execute Christ only during that same period of time. This is why the existence of Jesus at about A.D. 30 is not seriously questioned by historians today.

As we add up the evidence, then, we see that:

1. There was such a person as Jesus of Nazareth who was crucified by Pontius Pilate.
2. All the reliable accounts of the time date this event at A.D. 30 or 33.
3. Even without reference to any Christian accounts, we can date the event to the same time.
4. It would have been impossible to come up with such an accurate date for the fulfillment of Daniel's prophecy based on the knowledge available at the time of Christ's death!

THE BIG PICTURE

As we study Daniel 9, we begin to realize we have a prediction so remarkable that we are unable to give a convincing naturalistic explanation. The prediction was written hundreds of years before it was fulfilled, it is detailed and amazingly exact, and it could not have been faked by a false Christ or his followers. It is, in other words, exactly what God said he would provide—evidence that the Bible is his revealed Word and that Jesus is his Son.

As you read about the fulfillment of Daniel's prediction, you may be sensing that this is something unique. As you read on, you will find a growing body of evidence that will become increasingly persuasive. Eventually, you may have a desire to know more, to actually take a step of faith as described earlier. It's never too soon to take your search to God in person. God's love and his desire to enter into a personal relationship with you is what prompted him to reveal this evidence of his existence.

NOTES

1. Earlier in this same chapter Daniel says he read in the book of Jeremiah that God sent the nation of Israel into exile for seventy years because they had disobeyed the law of Moses. He discovered that God set the length of the

exile at seventy years because of the law of the seventh (Sabbath) year in Leviticus (also stated in 2 Chronicles 36:21). God had warned that if Israel disobeyed his covenant, he would scatter them "among the nations. . . . Then the land will enjoy its sabbath years all the time that it lies desolate and you are in the country of your enemies; then the land will rest and enjoy its sabbaths" (Leviticus 26:33-34). Daniel 9:11 also refers to this passage. Forsaking the sabbatical year was not the only sin Israel was guilty of during this period. They also committed sexual immorality, idolatry, and human sacrifice, to name a few. The sabbatical year seems to have been used to set the *length* of the exile, not the *fact* of the exile.

2. Scholars have challenged some of the predictions in Daniel in recent years, claiming that Daniel may have been written after some of the events predicted. If that were true, the book would really be only history, not prophecy. However, no one can claim Daniel 9 originated after the time of Christ. See a radical late-dating of Daniel to 160 B.C. in S. B. Frost, "Daniel," *The Interpreter's Dictionary of the Bible,* 1 (New York: Abingdon Press, 1962), pp. 761–768. This skeptical scholar admits, however, "That Daniel was widely recognized as scripture from the second and first centuries B.C. onward can be in no doubt" (762). Qumran (Q4) contained a commentary on Daniel. Also 1 Maccabees 2:59-60 refers to Daniel, and this book is no later in origin than 135 B.C. (S. B. Frost, "Daniel," *The Interpreter's Dictionary of the Bible,* 1, p. 763.) It should be clear, therefore, that Daniel could not have known what would happen in the first century A.D.

3. The decree mentioned in Daniel 9 relates to rebuilding the *city* of Jerusalem, not the temple. Also, the building of defenses is mentioned in Daniel 9:25: "It will be built again, with plaza and moat" (NASB). This is important, because these facts distinguish this decree from several

others that were issued in connection with rebuilding the temple only. However, even if we were to date the beginning of the vision to an earlier decree mentioned in Ezra 4:11-12, 23, the outcome would lead directly to the life and ministry of Jesus Christ. This is how scholars like J. Barton Payne understand the prediction. When handled this way, the ending date turns out to be A.D. 26. This, he argues, would have been the first year of Jesus' ministry. (J. Barton Payne, *Encyclopedia of Biblical Prophecy* [New York: Harper & Row, 1973], pp. 382–388.) This approach to the vision is certainly plausible. However, I believe that the approach outlined here is more accurate for the reasons given above and in note 8 below.

4. The Persian king's years were dated according to the "accession-year system." In this system ancients did not count the first partial calendar year of a king's reign, although we do count it. Because 465 would have been a partial year, Nisan (the first month of the year in their calendar) in the twentieth year of this king would have been in 444 B.C. The sometimes complicated procedures for reconciling ancient calendars is explained in detail in Jack Finnegan, *Handbook of Biblical Chronology: Principles of Time Reckoning in the Ancient World and Problems of Chronology in the Bible* (Princeton, N.J.: Princeton University Press, 1964), pp. 82–86.

5. Scholars such as Harold W. Hoehner have argued that this prediction points to the exact day of the Triumphal Entry of Christ. His conclusion rests on the assumption that when the day of the month is not given (as in Nehemiah) the first day should be assumed. Then the remainder is worked out to six digits, and compared to solunar tables that tell us what month this would indicate in A.D. 33. Harold W. Hoehner, "Chronological Aspects of the Life of Christ, Part 4: 'Daniel's Seventy Weeks and New

Testament Chronology,' " *Biblioteca Sacra,* 132, 525 (Jan.–Mar. 1975), pp. 46–65.

6. This is particularly true for the period before the beginning of the Seleucid era (312 B.C.). See a meticulous explanation in Jack Finnegan, *Handbook of Biblical Chronology,* pp. 21–123.

7. Josephus says, "This oracle [Daniel 9] certainly denoted the government of Vespasian, who was appointed emperor in Judea." (Flavius Josephus, *The Jewish War,* 4, 5, 4.) But Vespasian would have been forty years off the correct date. This is probably as close as they could come at that time.

8. Only the A.D. 33 date can explain the timid behavior of Pilate when threatened by the mob (John 19:12-16). Since he had been appointed by the Roman traitor Sejanus, who was found out in November A.D. 31, Pilate was in danger of being executed as a traitor. The purge of officials appointed by Sejanus was in full swing in A.D. 33. See Gary DeLashmutt, "Sejanus," *The Xenos Journal,* 2, 2, pp. 49–61. See also Harold Hoehner, "Chronological Aspects," *Biblioteca Sacra,* 132, 155 (Jan.–Mar. 1975) pp. 46–65.

9. Dates were based on the events going on in the Roman Empire at this time, particularly the acclamations voted to the emperor. Thus, a year might be described as "the year of the thirty-second imperator acclamation."

10. Josephus, *Jewish Antiquities,* 18, 3, 3. See also Tacitus, *Annals,* 15, 44, which includes the observation that Jesus was crucified by Pontius Pilate.

SEVEN
Isaiah's Remarkable Predictions

We have already seen some claims from the book of Isaiah. In the very section of Isaiah where God points to his ability to tell the future, a series of fascinating predictions serve as examples. The most interesting of these prophecies are known as the anonymous servant songs, four Hebrew poems that paint a picture of one known as "the servant of the Lord."[1]

The portrait of the servant is as follows: A savior will one day come who will be filled with the Spirit of God. He will begin his ministry in obscurity rather than with the majesty people would expect of such a savior. Indeed, this savior will be rejected by his own people. He will suffer persecution and torture. Although he will teach the Word of God, his contemporaries will believe that he is against God. Finally, the servant will be killed, but in dying, he will pay the price that the human race should have to pay for sin. After a period of time he will be raised from the dead, and multitudes will be brought into close relationship with God because of his work. Eventually, he will be crowned as a king, and even the other kings of the earth will be subject to him.

Notice that these prophecies were written hundreds of years before the time of Christ. Therefore, they constitute a preauthentication of Christ's ministry. Many aspects of the description were not under the control of Christ or any person. Also, the rabbis did not even understand these passages to be referring to the expected Messiah at the time Christ lived.[2] It would have been both impossible and pointless for Christ to deliberately fulfill these predictions. It would have been impossible because he had no way to obtain cooperation from the Roman and Jewish authorities who fulfilled the predictions by their actions. It would have been pointless because the predictions include the requirement that he must die.

The New Testament makes it clear that early Christians knew that these passages referred to Christ (see Matthew 8:17; 12:17-21; Acts 8:32-33). Some may wonder about the possibility that the New Testament authors falsified the history of Christ's life in order to make it seem like he fulfilled these prophecies. However, this explanation is not as simple as it seems. As we shall see later, modern scholars do not deny that the life and the death of Christ were real historical events. There is too much evidence, including sources outside of the Bible, to ignore. We find in these passages a remarkable description of the life and ministry of Jesus Christ written centuries before his birth. It is particularly striking to read Isaiah 53 from beginning to end. This passage is describing clearly, even to a first-time reader, the life of Jesus Christ.

THE MINISTRY OF ISAIAH'S ANONYMOUS SERVANT

1. He is filled with the Holy Spirit: "I will put my Spirit upon Him" (Isaiah 42:1; cf. Luke 4:1. All Scripture references quoted in this section are from the NASB).

2. He begins his ministry in obscurity and apparent failure.

   a. "In the shadow of His hand He has concealed Me . . . He has hidden Me in His quiver" (Isaiah 49:2).

   b. "I have toiled in vain" (Isaiah 49:4).

   c. "He has no stately form or majesty that we should look upon Him, nor appearance that we should be attracted to Him" (Isaiah 53:2).

3. The servant executes a prophetic or teaching ministry.

   a. "He will faithfully bring forth justice" (Isaiah 42:3). This indicates definitive decision or judgment.

   b. They "will wait . . . for His [oral] law" (Isaiah 42:4). *Torah,* here translated "law," also means teaching.

   c. "I will appoint you . . . a light to the nations" (Isaiah 42:6). He will be used to bring God's knowledge to Gentiles.

   d. His obedience results in the ability to teach faithfully and effectively (Isaiah 50:4).

4. The servant is humiliated and persecuted.

   a. The servant is voluntarily smitten, has his beard plucked, is spat upon, and is humiliated (Isaiah 50:6).

   b. His appearance is terribly marred (Isaiah 52:14).

   c. The servant is despised, forsaken, sorrowful, and grief-stricken (Isaiah 53:3).

   d. The servant is afflicted, bearing grief and sorrows (Isaiah 53:4).

   e. He is oppressed and afflicted (Isaiah 53:7).

   f. He is put to grief (Isaiah 53:10).

   g. He is crushed and scourged (Isaiah 53:5).

5. The servant is killed and buried (Isaiah 53:8-9). Note that the seemingly incomprehensible statement "His grave was assigned with

wicked men, yet He was with a rich man in His death" (53:9) is an accurate description of the burial of Jesus. As a victim of crucifixion, he should have been thrown into a common pit for criminals, but, instead, Joseph of Arimathea obtained Jesus' body from Pilate and placed it in a hand-hewn tomb—something only the rich could afford (John 19:38-41).

6. He atones for the sins of others by a substitutionary death (i.e., he dies in their place).

   a. "Thus He will sprinkle many nations" (Isaiah 52:15). This is a reference to ritual blood sprinkling as practiced in the Old Testament (cf. Exodus 29:16).

   b. The servant bears our griefs and sorrows (Isaiah 53:4).

   c. The servant is "pierced through for our transgressions, He was crushed for our iniquities; The chastening for our well-being fell upon Him" (Isaiah 53:5).

   d. "The Lord has caused the iniquity of us all to fall on Him" (Isaiah 53:6).

   e. "He was cut off from the land of the living, for the transgression of my people" (Isaiah 53:8).

   f. God renders the servant as a "guilt offering" for others' sins. This refers to Old Testament sacrificial ritual (Isaiah 53:10; cf. Leviticus 5:15).

g. "My Servant will justify the many, as He will bear their iniquities" (Isaiah 53:11).

h. "He poured out Himself to death, and was numbered with the transgressors; yet He Himself bore the sin of many, and interceded for the transgressors" (Isaiah 53:12).

7. He is raised from the dead: "He will prolong his days"—this, after the servant is dead and buried (Isaiah 53:10).

8. The servant's death leads to an ongoing ministry with his followers or "offspring" from all nations.

   a. The servant sets captives free (Isaiah 42:7; 49:9; 42:25).

   b. He will establish a new covenant with the Jews (Isaiah 42:6; 49:8).

   c. The servant will reconcile both Jews and Gentiles to God (Isaiah 49:5-6).

9. He is glorified.

   a. "Kings shall see and arise" (Isaiah 49:7)— standing up was (and is) a way of paying tribute. Kings never stood for a visitor—the visitor never sat down in the presence of a king.

   b. "Kings will shut their mouths on account of Him" (Isaiah 52:15).

   c. "I will allot Him a portion with the great" (Isaiah 53:12).

THE RESURRECTION OF JESUS

Those who deny the reality of the resurrection of Jesus have problems. No one denies that early Christians believed Jesus had risen from the dead. In fact, the resurrection of Christ was central to the Christian message from the earliest days. (See a summary of some of the evidence for this in J. P. Moreland, *The Secular City,* p. 161.) Further, we can determine that people held this belief in the very area where Jesus was buried. Why, then, did the authorities fail to exhume the body of Christ and demonstrate the falsehood of this sect they resented and persecuted so much? Why was there no veneration or commemoration of the tomb of Jesus as there generally is whenever a religious leader dies? Why are there no alternative explanations given in literature of the period explaining the "real" story (i.e., why Jesus really did not rise from the dead)?

One other question arises as well. We know those who claimed to be eyewitnesses of the death of Christ were subjected to persecution, including death. Why, if they knew there was no Resurrection, would they have allowed themselves to be put to death for a lie? Although others have claimed someone rose from the dead (even Elvis Presley!), how many have held to this claim in the face of persecution and death? It certainly seems that the disciples believed they had seen Christ alive. How could an entire group numbering in the hundreds come to believe something like this even to the point of persecution and death? These are some of the problems facing those who would deny the historical resurrection of Christ out of hand.

OTHER ASPECTS OF CHRIST'S LIFE PREDICTED

Many other prophecies in the Old Testament verify the claims of Christ; in fact, far too many to detail here. Although we don't have the space to examine the context and details of all of these passages, here is a partial list of some of the typical predictions and their fulfillments. Note that many of these features were not under Jesus' control, so he could not have "fulfilled" them on purpose if he were merely human.

Birthplace (Micah 5:2). The birthplace of Christ was named in advance. Only the small village of Bethlehem could be the birthplace of the Messiah. Note that events from the second coming of Christ are also mentioned in this passage, including the eventual takeover of the world.

Betrayal (Zechariah 11:12-14). The betrayal of Christ by Judas Iscariot is predicted in one passage where God is portrayed as a "foolish shepherd." For the purpose of communication, Zechariah the prophet enacted the betrayal and, remarkably, the actual figure of "thirty pieces of silver" is mentioned. God remarked with sad irony that this "magnificent sum" (the price of a slave) was the value the people placed on him.

The New Testament teaches that this divine drama was referring to the betrayal of Christ by Judas (Matt. 26:15). Notice the passage also predicts that the money would finally be thrown into the temple and given to a potter. This was fulfilled when Judas's money was used to buy land from a local potter after Judas's death.

Crucifixion (Psalm 22:6-18). Jesus' death by crucifixion was described in detail centuries before crucifixion had been invented! The details include the fact that his hands and feet were pierced, that he was naked, that his bones were being pulled out of joint, that his thirst was so intense that his tongue stuck to his jaws, that he was encircled by taunting persecutors as he died, and that men gambled for his clothing while he watched. Note that Jesus quoted the first verse of this psalm while on the cross: "My God, my God, why have you forsaken me?" No doubt he was calling the attention of the people to the fact that the well-known psalm was being fulfilled in their presence. Also, he literally was

being forsaken by God at that moment as the
judgment for human sin fell upon him.

Lineage (Matthew 1:1-16; Luke 3:23-38).   The
lineage of Christ was spelled out in detail hundreds of years before his birth. We also discover
a fascinating apparent contradiction here which
must have seemed irreconcilable. Yet all the
requirements were fulfilled. According to the
Old Testament, the Messiah must be:

- A descendant of Abraham (Genesis 12:3)
- A descendant of Isaac, not Ishmael (Genesis
  21:12)
- A member of the tribe of Judah rather than
  any of the other eleven tribes (Genesis 49:10)
- A descendant of David rather than any of the
  hundreds of other families in the tribe of
  Judah (Isaiah 9:6)
- A descendant of the kingly line of Solomon
  rather than any of the hundreds of other children in this huge family (2 Samuel 7:13)
- Yet, he could not be a descendant of Jeconiah,
  one of the kings in this very line (Jeremiah 22:28)

A careful reading of the two records of
Christ's lineage reveals that they are not the
same. Both agree up until the time of King David,
but Matthew says it was Solomon who gave rise
to the line of Christ, while Luke says it was

another son of David, Nathan, who gave rise to the line of the Messiah. The resolution of this quandary is found in verse 23 of Luke's account. There it says Jesus was "supposedly the son of Joseph, the son of Eli." In fact, this phrase could be taken to mean that Jesus was "supposedly the son of Joseph" (who, according to the claim of virgin birth, was not actually a blood relation of Jesus') but was really only the son of Mary. Eli would be Mary's father, not Joseph's father. (Women were routinely left out of these lists in the ancient world.) Therefore, the reason Matthew and Luke are different is that they trace Jesus' lineage through different parents.

As a result, Jesus fit all the requirements for the Messiah's lineage, even though those requirements seemed contradictory.

- He was in the line of David and was a blood descendant of David's through Mary
- He was not a blood descendant of Jeconiah who was accursed and disallowed from participating in this line
- He was entitled to be a part of the kingly line of David, including the right to be a king in that line, through inheritance from his adoptive father, Joseph

Can any other founder of a known religion point to a similar written record of his life already in existence hundreds of years before his birth? Would it have been possible, for instance, for Mohammad (the founder of Islam), Sakyamuni (Buddha), or Lao-tzu (the founder of Taoism) to point to a place in an already existing, widely known and read book and see there a listing of the unique features of his life?

No. No other founder of a world religion can point to such predictions to preauthenticate his ministry. Remember, Jesus had no control over the fulfillment of most of these prophecies. He could never have caused even the Romans to cooperate with any hoax. Besides, what motive would he have for dying by crucifixion if it was a hoax?

Jesus alone is able to say, "Everything must be fulfilled that is written about me in the Law of Moses, the Prophets and the Psalms."[3] The uniqueness of Christ is as real as the uniqueness of God himself, who said: "I am God, and there is no other. . . . I make known the end from the beginning, from ancient times, what is still to come" (Isaiah 46:9-10).

NOTES

1. The four passages are Isaiah 42:1-9; 49:1-13; 50:4-11; and 52:13–53:12. Although God makes other predictions involving his "servant Israel" in this part of Isaiah, these

four passages are clearly about a human servant rather than the nation of Israel for the following reasons:

a. Isaiah 49:1: The servant is called "from the womb" (NASB).

b. Isaiah 53:2-6: The contrast is made between "he" and "him" versus "we." The author (Isaiah) is Jewish, so the "we" must refer to the Jewish nation, or to the human race, including the Jewish nation. The servant is also contrasted to "my people" (the Jews) in 53:8.

c. The servant is said to be "the redeemer of Israel" (49:7, NASB), and he will "bring Jacob back to [God], in order that Israel might be gathered to Him . . . and to restore the preserved ones of Israel" (49:5-6).

d. The servant is called a "man" in 53:3 (see also 52:14; 53:8, 11).

e. Isaiah 53:8: The servant dies. But death is never predicted for the Jewish people. Rather, they will never pass away (cf. 55:9-10).

f. The servant is completely obedient and righteous, unlike the people of Israel, who are often chided for their sin, even in the servant songs themselves (see Isaiah 50:5 [NASB]: "I was not disobedient," and Isaiah 53:9 [NASB]: "He had done no violence, nor was there any deceit in His mouth").

2. This is probably one reason why the servant is never identified by name. It seems that God wanted to present the material in such a way that there could be no counterfeiting by false messiahs. Also, those opposing Christ would not realize they were actually assisting Christ and God when they put him to death. Only after the life and death of Christ did the full meaning of these prophecies become clear. Yet Christians are not misinterpreting the passages after the fact, because the passages can not be made to fit any other person or group. The rabbis had debated the meaning of these passages for centuries before the coming of Christ, but they could not reconcile this picture of the suffering and dying servant with the picture of

the triumphant "King Messiah" spoken of in passages such as Isaiah 9:6ff. The result was that some rabbis proposed that there were actually two Messiahs. We now know that there are not two Messiahs, but two comings of the same Messiah. See what the rabbis thought about these passages at the time of Christ in H. H. Rowley, *The Servant of the Lord and Other Essays on the Old Testament* (London: Latterworth Press, 1952), pp. 61–87.

3. See a complete collection of prophecies about Jesus in Herbert Lockyer, *All the Messianic Prophecies of the Bible* (Grand Rapids, Mich.: Zondervan, 1973).

EIGHT
Modern-Day Predictions

The life of Jesus fulfilled many prophecies in the Old Testament. However, many other kinds of predictions in the Bible also demonstrate its divine origin.

The New Testament and the Old Testament prophets agreed that history will move toward a climax. This climax will occur just before the personal return of Christ. Then history as we know it will come to an end, and God will supervise human society from that time on. This pattern could be called a linear view of history, because it has a beginning and an end.

Such a view of history is completely different from that held by many other religions. Most religions in the world hold that history is going through repetitive cycles. The cycles may be varying in length, but in general, religions tend to believe that human history will be either eternal or extremely long—some claim millions of years into the future.[1]

Most scholars are convinced that such circular views of history derive from the seasonal cycles in nature, and birth-fertility-death cycles. The religion apparently projects the course of nature onto history.[2] In agrarian societies where there had been little change for hundreds or thousands of years, such cycle theories were believable.

However, as human history has developed, it becomes increasingly clear that cyclical views are off-target. Human history is clearly moving in directions that have *never* occurred during a previous cycle. For instance, there has never been a period of highly developed technology or population density in alleged previous cycles of history. Instead of cycles, history is now clearly conforming to a pattern like that predicted in the Bible, as the graph on the next page shows.

The flow of history now increasingly appears to be moving toward a climax that will be different from anything before. The expected climax may also be quite near.

One of the most unique and convincing areas

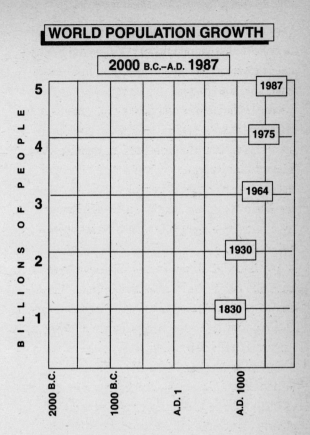

WORLD POPULATION GROWTH

2000 B.C.–A.D. 1987

BILLIONS OF PEOPLE

5

4

3

2

1

1987

1975

1964

1930

1830

2000 B.C.

1000 B.C.

A.D. 1

A.D. 1000

of prophecy in the Bible concerns events coming to pass in our own day. A few examples of current events predicted with accuracy in the Bible will help you understand why the Bible is not in the same class as other sources that claim to predict the future.

THE REGATHERING OF ISRAEL

In Luke 21 Jesus made predictions about his own time and about the flow of history until the end of the earth as we know it. He first predicted the destruction of Jerusalem. This destruction was so complete that not one stone of the temple was left standing (21:6). Expanding on this later, Jesus said,

> When you see Jerusalem being surrounded by armies, you will know that its desolation is near. . . . There will be great distress in the land and wrath against this people. They will fall by the sword and will be taken as prisoners to all the nations. Jerusalem will be trampled on by the Gentiles until the times of the Gentiles are fulfilled. (Luke 21:20, 23-24)

The passage predicts that Jerusalem would be surrounded by armies. It was fulfilled in A.D. 70. In that year, Titus Vespasian, later a Roman emperor, besieged Jerusalem and eventually burned the city and destroyed the buildings. The temple mount was completely leveled as Jesus had predicted. Many of the Jews in Jerusalem were killed by the Romans and the rest were deported to other areas, again as Jesus had predicted. Jerusalem fell under the power of non-Jews, as predicted by the statement that the city would be "trampled on by the Gentiles." This situation lasted until only recently.

But notice in verse 24 Jesus added an interesting phrase: "Until the times of the Gentiles are fulfilled." The word *until* implies that one day the city would again become a Jewish city. However, before Jerusalem could become a Jewish city, the Jews would have to be regathered from all of the countries to which they had been scattered. This is exactly what is predicted in several biblical passages, such as this one in Isaiah:

> In that day the Lord will reach out his
> hand a second time to reclaim the remnant
> that is left of his people from Assyria,
> from Lower Egypt, from Upper Egypt,
> from Cush, from Elam, from Babylonia,
> from Hamath and from the islands of the
> sea. (Isaiah 11:11)[3]

This reconstitution of a nation that had not existed for nearly two thousand years and whose people were living in other countries all over the world is absolutely without precedent in history. For many years even sympathetic readers doubted that this prediction should be taken literally, so unlikely was its fulfillment. Yet it has happened. In 1948 the nation of Israel was declared to exist by the United Nations. Then in 1967, Jerusalem finally was retaken by the Jews in accordance with Jesus' prophecy.[4]

This regathering was not just a precondition for the other events predicted in Luke 21. It was also pivotal in the program of God, because, according to verse 24, it signaled that "the times of the Gentiles are fulfilled." God's program for the Jewish people had been developing for thousands of years, as recorded in the Old and New Testaments. But God's stopwatch for biblical prophecy halted in A.D. 70 for an unspecified period of time called in this passage "the times of the Gentiles." However, when Jerusalem became a Jewish-controlled city in 1967, that stopwatch, after sitting still for nearly two thousand years, began to tick again! The events going on in Israel today are directly fulfilling prophecies uttered almost twenty centuries ago.

NUCLEAR WAR?

Fascinating and frightening predictions in both the New and Old Testaments foretell warfare during the final period of human history. According to Christ, warfare will increase in frequency and intensity, like the birth pangs of a woman in labor (Matthew 24:6-8). Amazingly, the accounts of war during the final period of human history sound identical to what we now recognize as nuclear war.

Referring to the final war of the world during the so-called "great tribulation" period, Jesus said that "if those days had not been cut short, no one would survive, but for the sake of the elect those days will be shortened" (Matthew 24:22).

This is a remarkable thing to say in a day when people were still fighting with spears! How could an ancient man even imagine a war that could kill everyone?

Elsewhere in the Bible this last war of the world is described in some detail.

In the Old Testament, Isaiah says that during "the day of the Lord" when there are "nations massing together . . . for war," live human beings will "look aghast at each other, their faces aflame." Survivors will become "scarcer than pure gold, more rare than the gold of Ophir" (Isaiah 13:4, 8, 12).[5]

Isaiah 24:6 predicts of the same period that "the earth's inhabitants are burned up, and very few are left."[6]

Revelation 9:16-18 predicts that one third of the population of the earth will be destroyed during a military episode that involves 200 million combatants!

These would have been absolutely preposterous predictions until our own day. The idea of 200 million combatants involved in one war is amazing!

To get an idea of the size of this figure, consider that there were fewer than 50 million in all services on all sides in World War II. Including civilian deaths, there were more than 50 million deaths in that war. This number of deaths is very high compared to even the most ferocious wars in the ancient world. Yet even 50 million deaths would fall far short of the predictions above. Today, one third of the earth's population would amount to about 2 billion deaths!

One of the most gruesome of these accounts is found in Zechariah 14. After a lengthy section referring to the last war of the world, which will center in the Middle East, it says:

> This is the plague with which the Lord will strike all the nations that fought against Jerusalem: Their flesh will rot while they are still standing on their feet, their eyes will rot in their sockets, and their tongues will rot in their mouths. (Zechariah 14:12)

Of course, flesh always rots after death. However, the important phrase to note in this statement is "while they are still standing on their feet." In other words, before they can even hit the ground dead, their flesh is literally flayed off their bones! This is reminiscent of some of the accounts from Hiroshima and Nagasaki. It is hard to imagine anything other than the heat of a nuclear blast that would be able to do what is described here.[7]

It's amazing to think that these predictions were all written thousands of years ago. How could these ancient men, who had never even seen gunpowder, imagine a war on such a scale as this? Truly, only the God of history himself could have known that man would eventually bring himself to the brink of self-annihilation in this manner.[8]

Readers of the Bible need an explaination for how these predictions could have been made. Was it a matter of coincidence? This hardly seems likely, since the matters predicted were outside of the experience of the authors. Besides, if they were coincidences, where are the other cases of coincidence in ancient Scriptures?

Predictive prophecy is named by God as an important vehicle of self-authentication, as we have seen. The more we study the predictive material itself, the more we realize that he also delivered the goods by producing a prophetic record without parallel in the world.

NOTES

1. Mircea Eliade, *Myths, Dreams and Mysteries* (London: Harvill Press, 1957), p. 49. See also his discussion of the universal "belief in a time that is cyclic, in an eternal return-ing, in the periodic destruction of the world and mankind to be followed by a new world and a new, regenerated man-kind." (Mircea Eliade, *Patterns in Comparative Religion* [New York: New American Library, 1974], p. 407.)

2. This is why, in most religions, the new-year festival is the premier festival of the year. (Harold Turner, "Holy Places, Sacred Calendars" in R. Pierce Beaver et. al., eds., *Eerdmans' Handbook to the World's Religions* [Grand Rapids, Mich.: Eerdmans, 1982], pp. 20–21.) Interestingly, in the Bible it is not clear that there even is a new year festival. Passover is in Nisan, which is the first month of the year (Exodus 12:2). However, it is on the fourteenth day of the month (Exodus 12:6). The new year held no great significance for the ancient Hebrews.

3. The "islands of the sea" probably refers to distant lands that lay beyond the ocean. See the prophecy of the dry bones in Ezekiel 37 for another example of prophecy that Israel would be regathered from all nations.

4. Note that Bible prophecy predicts both good and evil events. The fact that it predicts the retaking of Jerusalem by the Israelis is not in itself a moral commentary on all actions taken by the Israelis. In fact, some unjustifiable actions may well have occurred there. Jesus only says it will happen, not that it is morally correct. This is evident from the fact that the destruction of Jewish society by the Romans is also predicted in the same passage.

5. Although the context of the passage is the destruction of Babylon, Babylon has again taken on its frequent role as symbolic of the world system (compare Revelation 17–18, Isaiah 14). The prophecy is not just referring to the defeat

of the Babylonians by the Persians. This is evident for several reasons. First, the nations gathered for battle are multiple, not just one (verse 4). Second, mortal man becomes scarcer than gold. Finally, the nations come "from the farthest horizon," although Persia was a near neighbor to Babylon. The final destruction of Babylon is also connected with the end times in Revelation 17–18. The fact that God attributes the judgment to himself is not unusual, because he is allowing human agents to do it (Isaiah 7:20).

6. See verse 22: "In that day" God will judge the angels and mankind. This confirms that the passage is about the last days.

7. Again, God attributes this action to himself because he has the power to stop all sin if he so chooses. The fact that he does not constitutes a judgment on mankind. Natural forces are often at work in divine judgment, as seen for instance in Joel 1, where the swarm of locusts is "from the Lord." See also note 5 above. The context of this passage is war.

8. Some extrabiblical apocalyptic literature seems to parallel some of the predictions and even language found in Revelation or other biblical books. But remember, most of these depend directly on the Bible for their content. Nostradamus is a case in point.

NINE
Objections to Christianity

The prospect of establishing a relationship with God based on the claims of Christ is very attractive, as we have seen. However, there may be questions that keep some from taking such a step. In general, the answers to these questions are remarkably satisfying.

A brief outline of the chapter follows in order to clarify the line of reasoning:

What about other religions?
What about science and Christianity?
    Macroevolution
    Miracles
What about the existence of evil?
What about atrocities committed in the name of Christ?
What about hell?

WHAT ABOUT OTHER RELIGIONS?

Many of us love people who belong to different religions, and we feel uncomfortable claiming we know the truth while others do not. This may lead some of us to seek a way to accept all religions as true. When we say, "Why can't the other religions be different paths to the same summit?" we are expressing an accepting attitude toward others, which is good.

But before you jump on this bandwagon, ask yourself, are we really climbing a mountain here, or are we trying to discover what is true? What if you had some friends who believed cult leader David Koresh was Christ? Knowing what we know now, isn't it true that his followers were deceived by a false messiah? How about the followers of Jim Jones, the poisoner of Guyana? Today we can say without flinching that these sincere, convinced followers were sadly mistaken. How much better it would have been to convince them they were mistaken before it was too late!

When you think about it, a lot of people must be mistaken about religion. When the Hindu scriptures teach that souls are reincarnated, and Christianity teaches that "man is destined to die once, and after that to face judgment" (Hebrews 9:27), someone has to be wrong. Of course, they could both be wrong (if there is no afterlife), but they cannot both be right. This turns out to be the case in one area after another. The religions of the world contradict each other directly. This is true whether they are teaching on the nature of God, the nature of man, the way of salvation, or the meaning of history. These differences are particularly sharp when we compare the religions of the world to biblical Christianity. We have to decide which we think is right.

Such a search will turn up some interesting facts.

First of all, many religious scriptures appear to be based on speculation about nature. Another important source for sacred writings, in some cases, is the cultural background of the author(s).

For instance, an Egyptian religious myth that seems to be speculation teaches how clouds are created. According to this myth, the god Apsu masturbates and his semen issues in clouds.[1] Such a myth draws most of its insight from nature: the speculator has seen clouds rain on the fields, and the resulting fertility is one of the most commonly worshiped features of nature. The idea seems to be that, just as man's semen fertilizes the woman, the semen of the clouds brings fertility to the fields. The earth is often pictured as a mother and the bride of the sky for this reason.[2] Today we know that clouds are not created in this way and there are other reasons why fields are fertile.

How should the honest thinker today respond to such a myth? The answer is clear. Even if we had a relative or loved one who believed it, it simply is not true. This need not imply personal rejection of those who believe in false world-views or a sense of superiority on our part. In fact, the Christian is required to love those who are not Christians just as we love those who are (Matthew 5:46-47). Also, we can study religion to understand the meaning and value to those who believe it. There is no reason to deny that these beliefs bring comfort and joy to those who hold them. But the issue of truth cannot be over-looked.

Once we begin to admit that some religious teachings are false, we have to wonder where the line should be drawn. Should only the "worst" religions be rejected, such as those pro-moting human sacrifice or cannibalism?[3] Or should we also reject those teaching that women cannot enter the eternal state (Hinduism)[4] or that holy war is a moral virtue (Islam)?[5] The truth is that once we are prepared to say any religion is wrong, we have crossed the threshold into a critical assessment of all religions. We have admitted that all paths might *not* lead to God.

A critical approach to religion has a positive side too. When a view is falsifiable, it is also believable. Any claim that is not falsifiable cannot be discussed rationally. For instance, consider the claim that UFOs exist but they only appear when no one is watching. Such a claim can be neither verified nor falsified. It is, therefore, beyond discussion because it depends on blind faith. The realm of blind faith is also the realm of mindless faith.

On the other hand, no sophisticated view can be verified on *every* point. Even the most rigorous scientific outlook has to accept first principles based on implication and faith. For instance, no one knows what happened one second before the big bang. Yet something must have happened that we have never seen, have no name for, and cannot even describe. Is belief in a staggeringly powerful force that we have never seen and cannot name or describe any different from belief in God? Essentially, it is no different. Yet this doesn't mean a scientific worldview is unfalsifiable in general. Some areas are falsifiable, and others are not.

This is also the case in religion and religious scriptures. Although there may be some areas we can neither verify nor prove wrong, there are other areas we can. If the areas we can check prove false, we have no reason to believe the areas we cannot check. This is why we should reject any scripture's claims to truth if they contain verifiable, gross errors.

To summarize, it seems clear that we should view some religions and religious practices as false. If this is true with some, then it may be true with others in whole or in part as well. The final conclusion must be that we should try to evaluate religious teaching not only from the standpoint of the good feelings they create in their followers, but also from the standpoint of whether they are true. When religions contradict each other, we should seek a resolution, and this resolution may indeed favor one view over another.

To conclude that one religious doctrine or sacred scripture appears to be more believable need not be an act of personal arrogance or intolerance toward others. We make evaluations of this kind in other areas of life every day. If we are unable to evaluate some teachings at our present level of knowledge, we may remain neutral on those questions. However, this is still quite different from saying that two contradictory statements are both true.

There is no excuse at this point for becoming mentally lazy. Educators today complain about many in our culture who are unwilling to do the work of thinking through difficult issues. Sometimes people use the notion of moral relativism as an excuse for not thinking.[6] Fortunately, no such excuse is really necessary.

WHAT ABOUT SCIENCE AND CHRISTIANITY?

Another troubling area to modern thinkers is the area of science and Christianity. Does the Bible deny things that have been scientifically proven?

Today one can be a consistent scientific thinker and a committed believer in Jesus Christ and the Bible. Although Christians have resisted the advance of science at various points in history, nothing in the Bible necessarily contradicts any area of scientific consensus. We should note first of all that the Bible's worldview is in harmony with the first principles of science in that both believe in the uniformity of cause and effect in a real material world. This is different from most religions where every event has a spiritual cause or where the material world is not actually real. Perhaps no religious worldview is as harmonious with science as Christianity. Most philosophers of science agree: It's no accident that modern science arose in Christian-influenced Europe.

On the other hand, Christianity believes that, while cause and effect are real and account for most events, there is also the real possibility of direct divine intervention at any given time. Therefore, Christians can accept scientific explanations for natural events while also accepting biblical explanations for supernatural events.

Certain areas of tension remain, however, between modern scientific consensus and biblical teaching. The main areas of tension are macro-evolution and the existence of miracles.

Macroevolution. Most evangelicals today believe that some types of evolution have occurred, but only within limits. This accords well with what science has uncovered in the fossil record. While we can demonstrate considerable microevolution (smaller changes or adaptations in species), there are large gaps in the fossil record that we now realize will never be filled. In Genesis, we read that God created living organisms in such a way that each reproduced "according to their kinds" (Genesis 1:11, 21, 24). The passage gives no definition for the word *kind* in any scientific sense, and therefore the scope of the term is a matter of interpretation. Perhaps God created only a limited number of "kinds," or general categories of creatures, and a process of natural selection has caused the variety we see today.

Perhaps these categories were not all created at the same time, but were gradually introduced over many years. Bible scholars have shown several ways to see this in the text of Genesis. Others argue that the creation in Genesis is actually a re-creation of a world that already existed but had been substantially destroyed. Still others believe there is no need to see any passage of time in the biblical creation account.

All biblical Christians agree on one point: The human race was a product of direct divine intervention, not merely natural process.

This point must be true if people have souls or spirits. Obviously, no process of biological evolution could ever produce a spiritual entity that would survive the death of the physical organism. We cannot believe in a personally conscious afterlife unless we acknowledge a nonbiological, nonmaterial dimension to humans. This nonmaterial entity could only derive from a nonmaterial source: God himself. The Bible explicitly teaches this in Genesis 2:7 and elsewhere. Of course, the question of whether humans have a spirit is not an issue science can speak to, since such a spirit is not measurable or observable by material measures.

Miracles. Some scientists have thrown doubt on the notion of miracles, such as Jesus healing or walking on water. They claim such events are implausible or unlikely because they cannot be repeated and observed.

It should be clear from the outset that this question is the same as the question of the existence of God. It would be ridiculous to say that God exists, and then proceed to say he can't do this or that. The issue of the existence of God has to be settled in our minds before we can address the plausibility of miracles. No person who denies that the supernatural exists will ever believe in miracles. Neither should we have any trouble with miracles once we admit that a supernatural God exists.

WHAT ABOUT THE EXISTENCE OF EVIL?

The world manifests evil and injustice. This fact gives rise to the most important objection people raise to the idea of a Creator God. Simply stated, if the Creator of the world is good, why is his creation so often bad?

Biblical Christianity stands out as the most satisfying explanation for the presence of evil. The Bible starts with the claim that God built free choice into humans at the beginning. This freedom is the center post of the biblical explanation. Yet some still think we cannot effectively distance God from evil simply by saying that the human race has (or did have) the capability of free choice. Was it not an immoral decision on God's part to create something that he knew would result in such trouble?

This is a good question, but we should look at the broader picture for the answer. Clearly, God made a decision to create freedom even though it would lead to pain and suffering. This constitutes a value judgment: freedom was more important than the avoidance of evil. But why should God value freedom so highly?

We don't know the full answer to this last question, but we do know part of the answer.

Personhood requires freedom. There can be no personality where there is no free choice. Suppose you built a robot that could speak. Perhaps you program it to say "I love you" when you push a button. You push the button several times, but you feel no pleasure from hearing the statement. That's because this statement is not the product of a thinking, choosing person. The robot does not love you; it is only repeating what you programed it to say. You might as well talk to yourself.

This simple illustration shows the importance of freedom. Without freedom, there would be no personality other than God. When we say "free choice," we mean truly free, not just free in word only. Therefore, if God created any freedom, it must be possible to misuse that freedom.

Some atheistic authors have tried to argue that God should have created people with freedom who would always choose to do good. But this is just like saying that God should have created a square triangle. Any effort to describe freedom that has only one choice is an exercise in absurdity. These two concepts are in direct contradiction. Therefore, we see the trade-off between two desirable things: on one hand personality, and on the other, an evil-free universe. God has rejected the alternative of preprogrammed machines in favor of people with personalities like his own.

Why so long?   Why, after people chose evil, didn't God put an end to the problem and start over? This option seems reasonable enough, but upon more reflection, we realize it would be a simplistic and dangerous solution.

First, we need to realize that revolution—the rejection of divine leadership—is based on suspicion of God's character. In Genesis, for instance, Satan told Eve that the real reason God forbade them to eat certain fruit was that he was unwilling to let humans become like himself (Genesis 3:5). This shows that Satan has brought accusations against the character of God, charging that he is not loving and that he is holding out on his creatures and repressing them. Satan must have

made a similar claim to the host of other creatures that inhabit the universe, because we know
that some of them also joined his revolution
(Revelation 12:3-4, 7, 9).

What would it look like to the citizens of the
universe if every time someone revolted, God
immediately zapped them out of existence?
Wouldn't this tend to confirm that God is unlov-
ing and self-serving? Clearly, the simple solution
is not as workable as it seems. It would probably
be only a matter of time before another revolt
occurred, followed by another purge. This might
continue throughout the course of eternity!

God decided to deal with the problem of the
misuse of freedom once and for all. Instead of
immediately terminating the revolution, he
decided to let it develop fully. Today, through
the futility of human history and through the
self-sacrificial intervention of Christ, evidence is
accumulating that will render revolution implausible in the future. God has delayed forceful
intervention in our history so that evil can be
taken out of the way once and for all, rather
than in an endless series of revolts and judg-
ments (Hebrews 9:12, 26, 28; 10:10).

Viewed this way, the value judgment God
made was not irrational at all. This explains
why God would not put an immediate end to
evil. Of course, according to the Bible, God will

eventually put an end to the revolt. This will occur when Jesus returns. Before that time, though, there are key objectives to be reached. We have already seen that hundreds and even thousands of years were necessary to develop the verifiable first coming of Christ. Now God is accomplishing other strategic ends, including winning a large group of people from all over the world. These people will serve as permanent witnesses to both the vanity of revolt against God and the kindness of God as seen in Christ's willingness to die for us. Thus, Paul said his job was:

> To make plain to everyone the administration of this mystery, which for ages past was kept hidden in God, who created all things. His intent was that now, through the church, the manifold wisdom of God should be made known to the rulers and authorities in the heavenly realms, according to his eternal purpose which he accomplished in Christ Jesus our Lord. (Ephesians 3:9-11)[7]

Is it fair? How can it be right for us to have to suffer today for a decision made at the time of the creation of the human race? Besides, evils such as storms and earthquakes are not the direct result of human choice. Why then are many people allowed to suffer without cause on their part?

To understand this, we need to realize that Adam decided to throw off completely God's leadership. According to the Bible, this choice had repercussions. When Adam rejected God's leadership he rejected all God's protection and control over nature. Humankind was saying, "We can take care of ourselves without you." Unfortunately, man cannot take care of himself. He cannot control the environment, hostile microbes, or even his own nature.

Still, why should Adam's decision affect us today? Wouldn't it only be fair to let each of us make our own decision?

To answer this, we have to come to grips again with the nature of free choice. Free choice is not only responsible, it's also significant. If someone decided to push the button for a nuclear war, the choice of one person would affect everyone for many years to come, and the effect would be unfair. Yet, what is the alternative? Clearly, if only those choices are allowed that do not adversely affect anyone else, there would be virtually no freedom at all! This is because one of the things we can choose to do is to be unfair and to harm other people.

Where should the line be drawn? God drew the line at total freedom with regard to this world. To put it differently, humans were free to do whatever they were able to do by themselves. This level of freedom was a high level indeed, and, to God, having such freedom was better than avoiding the possibility of evil.

How to view current events. The upshot of this scenario is that we cannot expect fairness in a fallen world. The world would be fair and benign if God were in direct control of it, as he will be when Christ returns. However, in the meantime, we are alienated from God to a terrible degree. "The whole creation has been groaning as in the pains of childbirth," as it awaits the day when "the creation itself will be liberated from its bondage to decay and brought into the glorious freedom of the children of God" (Romans 8:21-22).

Let's return to an earlier question, What is the Christian explanation for specific tragedies that occur? So often we hear people in sorrow at times of death or other tragedies asking why. This question is usually a plea for justice. "Why did God do this?" might be the full question. The Christian answer, in most cases, would be that the event has occurred as a result of uncontrolled cause and effect. Christians share this point of view with modern science.

It is usually a mistake to attribute illness and

death to the wrath of God. Jesus indicated this when he commented on tragedies that occurred during his time. He affirmed that the people killed by the collapse of a tower were no different from anyone else. Why, then, did they die? Because they were standing under the tower when it fell. (See Luke 13:1-5.) Christ resisted the rabbinic tendency to attribute illness, poverty, and misfortune to the justice of God. Even though there are times when God may judge people through calamity in this life (Isaiah 45:7), this is not the norm. The wicked often prosper more than the righteous, and innocent babies suffer. The Christian thinker realizes these events are a product of the general fallen status of the world.

God permissively allows cause and effect to carry on, awaiting a time when he will take control of the situation. In the meantime, he will intervene in life periodically on his own initiative and will intervene even more often when invited to do so by one of us in prayer (James 5:16).

The Bible's view of cause and effect is much more believable than systems of thought that try to explain everything on the basis of divine action. These other systems seek to explain why everything that happens is really fair after all, when it clearly isn't. Biblical Christianity, on the other hand, agrees with the findings of modern science. While affirming the possibility that God may elect to intervene in history, biblical Christianity holds that cause and effect account for most events in the natural world.

WHAT ABOUT ATROCITIES COMMITTED IN THE NAME OF CHRIST?

The Christian church has done some great things in its history, and many vital, healthy churches today meet the needs of their people. However, modern Christians have some questions to answer about problems in the history of the church.

In fact, the history of the "Christian" church has been quite disappointing from a biblical point of view. Examples abound of atrocities committed in the name of Christ. Through much of Christian history, opponents of the church have been subjected to torture and cruel death.[8] Then there were the religious wars, including the Crusades, which resulted in hundreds of thousands of deaths under the banner of the Cross and often to the sound of hymns of thanksgiving.[9] Praises to God were also sung during genocidal massacres of entire Jewish communities long before Hitler.[10] During Hitler's time, much of the German Lutheran church, the Roman Catholic church, and even some of the

American churches supported his regime.[11] How could such events happen if Christianity is a religion of truth and love?

To understand this, we need to look at the development of certain trends in church history that eventually took part of Christianity far away from what God intended it to be.

The early period. Early church leaders, fearing heresy, began to carefully control the theological material to which people had access.[12] In addition, the pressure of persecution tended to foster legalism, hyper-strictness, and anti-Semitism.[13]

Later, when Christianity was embraced by the Roman government in the 300s, money and power began to flow into the church.[14] The faith described in the Bible was distorted by the addition of popular superstition. Sometimes confused or corrupt leaders even replaced the biblical message completely with a message that was more suitable for attaining control of the situation.[15]

One of the earliest misfortunes in church history was the abandonment of the grammatical-historical method of interpreting the Bible.[16] Instead, the narratives were converted into allegories with symbolic meaning. This left the interpreter free to assign his own interpretation to the text. Since anyone could assign his own meaning, the Bible tended to lose authority. Instead, a new authority was appointed to determine which allegory was appropriate in each case.

The loss of popular access to the Bible. This new authority was the church hierarchy, which asserted that they alone were authorized to interpret the Bible.[17] The people were discouraged from independent Bible study, and they gradually began to relate more to icons (holy pictures and statues) and temples than they did to the written Word.[18] The church excused this change by pointing out that the people were illiterate and that it would be divisive to allow each person to reach his own conclusion about Scripture's meaning. But this was not really a sufficient answer because oral societies are able to learn and study the written Scriptures through public reading (1 Timothy 4:13). Besides, the church should have taken an interest in teaching more people to read. Later, during the Protestant Reformation, it was the church that pushed for universal compulsory education so people could read the Bible.[19]

Once the Bible was taken out of the hands of the average person, no one could prevent teachings alien to the Bible from entering the church. Eventually the church began to claim openly that it could generate new "divinely inspired" material apart from any biblical authority.[20] The church claimed more and more authority for itself, and, eventually, opposition to the church became a capital crime in Europe. Hundreds of thousands of religious dissidents (including Jews) were tortured and killed in Europe during the medieval period.[21]

Modern readers find it hard to understand how there came to be such a disparity between the Christian church and the Bible upon which it was supposedly based. But once biblical authority is subjected to human authority, anything can happen. Although the Protestant movement in the 1500s corrected many of these excesses, the Reformed, Lutheran, and Anglican churches continued to practice the power tactics of their predecessors. Dissenters and Jews were frequently persecuted and killed in the name of God.[22]

Responding to abuses. Today, some churches are still openly evil, as when they teach race hatred and group suicide, or when they bilk money from the ignorant for greedy church leaders. Others are merely ridiculous, as when they engage in superstitious practices and doctrines or various extrabiblical types of ritualism, like snake handling. Of course, other churches are completely innocent of these kinds of abuse.

Why would God allow his church to go so far astray, and how can we speak of Christianity without also speaking of the Christian church? Is it really possible to divorce the biblical message from the historical church?

The answers to these questions can be found in the Bible itself. Jesus predicted there would be many impostors invading the church:

> Watch out for false prophets. They come to you in sheep's clothing, but inwardly they are ferocious wolves. By their fruit you will recognize them. Do people pick grapes from thornbushes, or figs from thistles? Likewise every good tree bears good fruit, but a bad tree bears bad fruit. . . . Thus, by their fruit you will recognize them. Not everyone who says to me, "Lord, Lord," will enter the kingdom of heaven. (Matthew 7:15-17, 20-21)

According to this passage, Christ teaches that professed Christian leaders cannot be trusted based merely on their word. We have to evaluate the truthfulness of any leader by examining that person's morality ("fruit") and faithfulness to the biblical message.[23] In cases where church leaders are involved in violence, lying, or immorality, they have obviously failed this test.

Observe in the passage cited above that Christ puts the burden on the individual believer to distinguish the true teachers from the false. This means we will never reach a point where we can safely say, "I let my priest or pastor figure out what is right in theological matters." Paul also warned Timothy that fidelity to the Bible would be an essential test:

> Preach the Word. . . . For the time will come when men will not put up with sound doctrine. Instead, to suit their own desires, they will gather around them a great number of teachers to say what their itching ears want to hear. They will turn their ears away from the truth and turn aside to myths. (2 Timothy 4:2-4)

Observe also that the Bible was not written to theologians or church leaders (with the exception of the Pastoral Epistles), but to the common people in local fellowships. Even if a group was illiterate, Paul ordered that his letters be read to "all the brothers" (1 Thessalonians 5:27).[24] Therefore, although we should listen to the scholarship of leaders, we should never shirk our responsibility to interpret and apply the Bible. Indeed, how could it be otherwise? If God protected us from all deception, he would have to completely disrupt the freedom of the human race.

In the final analysis, we need to make a clear

distinction between the teachings of the Bible and the practices of those claiming to follow the Bible. There is such a thing as deception, and the enemy of human souls will counterfeit the truth as much as possible.

We should not forget the important exceptions to the lamentable trend in the church through history. Christians have contributed to, and led, a number of important social changes. For example, most historians see the Christian church as central (though tardy) in the abolition of human slavery. Universal education is a legacy of the Reformation. Many loving Christian communities have contributed positively to society. Unfortunately, these have not been as numerous as we would like.

Regardless of how people may have misused the truths in the Bible, the Bible says that when we come before God, we will answer to the standard of truth (Romans 2:2). It is to this truth, found in God's revelation, the Bible, not to strange churches that have sprung up over the years, that we should listen.

WHAT ABOUT HELL?

The God revealed in the Bible is said to be just. In other words, he is not able to observe evil passively without eventually doing something about it. His reaction to evil is called judgment, and we have come to refer to God's punishment as hell.

Hell is a disturbing concept for anyone who thinks seriously about it. This is because hell is not remedial but retributive. In other words, the idea is not to *fix* people, but to *repay* them for what they did in fair measure. The concept of hell cannot be made benign, because it is truly terrible. However, if this is reality, we have to come to grips with it. A few points will help here.

First, the Bible teaches that God grants to everyone what is called "common grace." Common grace is a gift that enables people to know God is there and that he is the personal Creator of the world. Romans 1 says:

> What may be known about God is plain to [people], because God has made it plain to them. For since the creation of the world God's invisible qualities—his eternal power and divine nature—have been clearly seen, being understood from what has been made, so that men are without excuse. (Romans 1:19-20)

This passage teaches that those who have not heard the Bible have access to two sources of insight about God. One is within ourselves ("it is evident *within* them" NASB, emphasis mine). This is also referred to by Christ when he said that he would "draw all men" to himself (John 12:32). In other words, God sees to it that everyone knows within themselves that they are a spiritual being and that they need God. We have a clear sense that we are different from other biological organisms. Our sense of love, our love of art and beauty, and our inner sense that there is such a thing as morality all suggest we are personal beings. This is why God says it is evident within us that we came from a personal spiritual source.

The other source is "what has been made," which refers to nature. We already saw why honest reflection on the rest of nature suggests the presence of a Creator God. On the basis of these two things, Paul says people are without excuse. What does this mean?

Actually, we don't know exactly how God will deal with those who have not heard the gospel. We do know, however, that according to the biblical view of justice we are responsible for what we know, not for what we don't know. This is why infants are apparently always taken to heaven.[25] Therefore, if these people are "without excuse," it must mean they are able to do something that would cause God to be willing to apply the death of Christ to them. The Bible does not say what response is required in the case of those without access to the Bible, but it does rule out quite a few possibilities. In verse 25 of the same chapter, it says God would not accept those who "worshiped and served created things rather than the Creator." Apparently, everyone knows better than to worship nature. The desire to worship nature probably stems from a desire to avoid the God *behind* nature.

Unfortunately, we see little evidence that many people are responding to this common grace in areas where the Christian gospel is unknown, although there are some outstanding exceptions.[26] At the same time, it is nice to know God is active in reaching out to all people. The biblical Christian has to trust that people will be treated fairly by a fair God.

Even with the notion of common grace, the main problems with hell are unresolved. To fairly evaluate the biblical position on hell, we have to consider the alternatives to the biblical view.

Alternative views.   The idea of hell is deplorable. But what is the alternative?

According to the atheistic worldview, there is no afterlife at all, so the question is moot. To the atheist, everyone—the evil and the best people as well—shares the same fate of oblivion.

The Eastern mystic foresees no better fate. For them, the devotee must try to escape *maya*—the veil of tears, suffering, and illusion—in an effort to reach *moksha, nirvana,* or similar concepts. Although everyone is said to eventually make it to this goal, it would be a big mistake to connect these ideas of afterlife with our Western concept of heaven.

In biblically inspired religions, individuals continue to exist and know who they are in the afterlife. People are able to relate to each other in a personal way in the new heaven and new earth described in the Bible. But in Eastern monistic conceptions, this is not the case. According to the Eastern scriptures, the individual is merged with the universal consciousness, and becomes a part of what is called the "All" or "universal emptiness." You, as a distinct person with feelings and thoughts, cease to exist according to this view.[27] The Eastern monistic concept of "heaven" is similar to what we in the West would call *oblivion.* The main benefit one gains from entering this final state is that one no longer has to return through reincarnation to the material world of suffering. This prospect is quite depressing, when the best one can expect from religion is to escape the agony of reincarnation and rebirth in *maya.*[28]

In the case of tribal polytheism and other theistic views, a personal heaven exists. This follows quite naturally from the idea that God is personal. On the other hand, these religions almost invariably teach that there is also a hell. Therefore, they agree with Christianity in this area. However, the difference is that entrance into heaven is based on belonging to a privileged class of people or on the performance of religious laws, as seen earlier.

Heaven without hell? In modern times, some Christian and Jewish theologians have moved toward a view that a personal heaven exists but that no personal hell exists. This view is called universalism, because it teaches that God will save all people somehow. However, this view has a number of problems that render it unacceptable.

First, if there is to be no judgment, then we will be in heaven with an unrepentant Hitler. If this is the case, one must ask some urgent questions. On the one hand, if God is unconcerned about the difference between good and evil, what sort of heaven can we expect? If he is not averse to evil, this doesn't bode well for any of us. We would then be dealing with a God who treats evil and good alike. In fact, the difference between these two would be more or less academic.

On the other hand, perhaps people aren't held

responsible for evil under the universalist system because they couldn't help but do evil. Perhaps, according to universalists, God thinks Hitler was raised in a way that forced him to commit atrocities. However, if that were true, who was the author of such an environment? Indeed, God himself must be culpable! Certainly, if the people are not responsible, someone else must be. The only plausible candidate here is God.

Why would a universalist God allow evil to continue? Without the existence of free will and the responsibility that comes with it, what is to be gained by simply watching people helplessly suffer? If God will send us all to everlasting reward anyway, why delay further? Why put us through seventy years of pain first? If suffering in this life is without positive effect, it suggests that God may even be sadistic.

If, however, we admit free will exists, we cannot deny human responsibility. It would be absurd to claim that we make the decisions, but God is responsible. *We* must be responsible if our choices are free, because no one is making us do what we do. On the other hand, as stated earlier, the Bible indicates that God does not hold responsible babies or others who cannot choose. We cannot separate free choice from responsibility.

This is why God judges. According to the Bible, people *are* responsible for the situation on earth, both corporately and individually. Also, as we have seen, temporal suffering is not usually a result of divine judgment. This is why infants may suffer temporally, but they will not go to hell.

Here is another problem with universalism: No known Scripture teaches this idea of a non-judging, personal God. The authority behind this view comes from people's own imagination. The universalist God is a product of late twentieth-century European/American culture, where we want our authorities to be amoral, accepting, and nonjudgmental. But is it reasonable to think I could create a new religion with tenets that please me, and feel that because I believe it, it will actually be true? If this were possible, everyone could simply describe a religion they like, and appropriate gods and afterlives would spring into existence as a result! Unless we have evidence outside of ourselves that a certain view is true, we are simply engaging in wishful thinking. This is the case with universalism.

Setting the right sentence.   So what should the penalty for evil be? Those who have experience with prisons discover most prisoners believe they are being treated unfairly. Perhaps some of them are, but it's unlikely that most of them are. Instead, we are seeing here a feature of human nature. People tend to think what they do is not very bad and does not deserve much punishment. We can see this is an inborn characteristic by observing young children when they get in trouble. Nobody has to show them how to blame others, to minimize their own wrongdoing, and to complain that they are being treated too harshly.

This is probably why we don't let criminals set their own sentences. They would probably go too soft on themselves.

God doesn't let us set our own sentences either. He has determined that certain sentences are appropriate for various sins. We are told that at the judgment day, he will justify his choices for all to see. We don't know exactly how this will work, but we do know the consequences of divine judgment will be eternal.

The really remarkable thing is not that God judges, but that he has undergone his own judgment! Christ has made it possible for everyone to escape the sentence of hell at his expense.

Now we find ourselves in a situation similar to a man who took an ocean liner from New York to London. In the fog off Greenland, the ship struck an iceberg and sank. The man found himself in the water beginning to freeze to death, when a lifesaver on a rope came sailing toward him out of the fog.

If the man looked away and said, "I don't need that, because there is nothing wrong with me," his reaction would be similar to that of the universalist or the Eastern mystic.

The man might say, "I did nothing to get into this situation, and I refuse to legitimize the situation by admitting I need that lifesaver. I demand to be bodily removed instantly!" Such a response is not unlike that expressed by the nontheist who feels too morally outraged by issues like hell or the existence of evil to appreciate what God is offering.

The only sane approach is to gratefully seize what we can understand now (the lifesaver) and seek explanations later for the part we cannot understand.

NOTES

1. This myth is from an inscription inside the pyramids of Mernere and Pepi II, dating from about the twenty-fourth century B.C. Available in translation by Phyllis Ackerman, "The Dawn of Religions," Vergilius Ferm, *Forgotten Religions* (New York: The Philosophical Library, 1950).

2. "The divine couple, Heaven and Earth . . . are one of the *leitmotiven* [central motifs] of universal mythology." (Mircea Eliade, *Patterns in Comparative Religion,* p. 240. See his whole discussion on "Earth, Woman, Fertility,"

pp. 239–264.) See also Mircea Eliade, *Myths, Dreams and Mysteries,* pp. 155–189. See many other examples of earth-mother cults in James G. Frazer, *The Golden Bough,* pp. 39–423.

3. Eliade, perhaps the most renowned comparative religion scholar of this century, takes relativism to its logical extreme when he says, "It should always be remembered, before passing judgment upon cannibalism, that it was founded by divine Beings." And, "Before pronouncing a moral judgment upon these customs, one should remember this—that to kill a man, and eat him or preserve his head as a trophy, is to imitate the behavior of the Spirits, or of the gods. Thus, replaced in its own context, the act is a religious one, a ritual." (Mircea Eliade, *Myths, Dreams and Mysteries,* pp. 47, 200.)

4. Denise L. Carmody and John T. Carmody, *Ways to the Center* (Belmont, Calif.: Wadsworth Publishing Co., 1984), p. 89.

5. *Koran* 9:5; 4:76; 2:214; 8:39.

6. Allan Bloom, *The Closing of the American Mind* (New York: Simon & Schuster, 1987).

7. The mention of secrecy in verse 9 is interesting, but unfortunately the reason for secrecy lies outside the scope of this book. Suffice it to say that God did keep his purpose secret until the last minute, as part of his strategic plan of war with Satan. This desire for secrecy actually led to the biggest mistake Satan ever made—conspiring to kill Christ.

We would argue that the master rebel did not realize this was exactly what Christ wanted (1 Corinthians 2:8). God created confusion and secrecy by deliberately omitting to mention in the Old Testament prophecies that there would be two comings of King Messiah. Also, this need for secrecy explains why passages we studied earlier, like the servant songs in Isaiah, do not come out and say they refer to the Messiah.

God set up the predictive material in such a way that, up until the minute Christ died, it was hard to say to whom these predictions referred. But one minute after Christ's death, it was impossible to deny the clear fulfillment! See also Luke 24:44-48; John 12:32-34; 16:25; Romans 16:25; 1 Peter 1:12.

8. During the Inquisition, torture of children and the aged was to be kept light, but only pregnant women were exempt, and then only until after delivery. Death at the burning stake for heretics was carried out by the secular authorities because "the church could not shed blood." (Ronald Finucane, "Persecution and Inquisition," *Eerdmans' Handbook to the History of Christianity* [Grand Rapids, Mich.: Eerdmans, 1977], p. 31. This entire section is an excellent and fair explanation of the problem of persecution during this period; see pp. 34–323.)

9. After marching around Jerusalem "barefoot, singing penitential hymns," the crusaders broke into the city. "There followed a horrible bloodbath. All the defenders were killed as well as many civilians. Women were raped, and infants thrown against walls. Many of the city's Jews had taken refuge in the synagogue, and the crusaders set fire to the building with them inside. According to an eyewitness, at the Porch of Solomon horses waded in blood." (Justo L. Gonzalez, *The Story of Christianity,* vol. 1 [New York: Harper & Row, 1984], pp. 1, 295–296.)

10. For an excellent collection of source readings in translation from this period (many written by church officials), see Jacob R. Marcus, ed., *The Jew in the Medieval World,* (Antheneum, N.Y.: Antheneum, 1969), pp. 155–158. A typical incident of church persecution involved the Jews of Passau. Under torture they admitted that they had obtained several hosts (communion wafers) and "that when they had

stabbed the hosts, blood flowed from them; that the form of a child arose; and that when they tried to burn the wafers in an oven two angels and two doves appeared." Four of the arrested Jews converted to Christianity and were treated kindly as a result: they were merely beheaded. The rest were torn with hot pincers and burned alive. Examples of such atrocities abound in the history of the church. Marcus includes a score of typical examples, such as the burning of over two thousand Jewish men, women, and children in Strasbourg in 1349 (p. 45). These examples are included because some church members today have difficulty admitting the reality of church-caused atrocities. Note that the accounts mentioned here were not written by enemies of the church, but are original accounts written by clergymen at the time and correlated with parallel accounts.

11. For example, at the time of the Weimar republic, "It is estimated that seventy to eighty percent of the Protestant pastors allied themselves with . . . *the Deutschnational Volkspartei.*" This party advocated "every expression of justifiable anti-Semitism." (David Rausch, *Legacy of Hatred: Why Christians Should Not Forget the Holocaust* [Chicago: Moody Bible Institute, 1984], pp. 50–51.)

12. See a typical early response to heresy by Ignatius of Antioch, where he reminds them among other things to "let no man do anything connected with the Church without the bishop," and, "He who does anything without the knowledge of the bishop does [in reality] serve the devil." That the pressure of heresy was the driving force behind this restrictive new teaching is evident in this passage and in the letter to the Philadelphians: "Keep yourselves from those evil plants which Jesus Christ does not tend [heretics]. . . . For as many as are of God and of Jesus Christ are also with the bishop." He repeatedly calls on the people to "be subject to the bishop as to the Lord." (Ignatius of Antioch, "Letter to the Smyrnaeans," "Letter to the Trallians,"

and "Letter to the Philadelphians," in Alexander Roberts and James Donaldson, eds., *The Ante-Nicene Fathers,* vol. 1 [Grand Rapids, Mich.: Eerdmans, 1985], pp. 66, 80, 89–90.)

13. A good survey of this period is M. A. Smith, *From Christ to Constantine* (Downers Grove, Ill.: InterVarsity Press, 1971).

14. Williston Walker, *A History of the Christian Church,* fourth edition, (New York: Scribners, 1985), pp. 129–130.

15. See a discussion of these developments in Kenneth Scott LaTourette, *A History of Christianity,* vol. 1 (New York: Harper & Row, 1975), pp. 208–218.

16. A grammatical-historical interpretive method seeks the meaning using the rules of grammar in the original language, colored as appropriate by the historical context. It allows for figures of speech and idiomatic expression. Symbolism is only accepted when the text clearly intends to be symbolic. The advent of allegorical interpretation coincided with the intrusion of Platonic philosophy into the thinking of the church. It also stemmed from a desire to present the Old Testament as a Christian book. See a fair but critical treatment in Bernard Ramm, *Protestant Biblical Interpretation* (Grand Rapids, Mich.: Baker, 1970), pp. 23–45. Clement of Alexandria is credited with popularizing the allegorical approach to the Bible and for incorporating Greek philosophy into Christian theology. See his explanation in "The Stromata," *The Ante-Nicene Fathers,* vol. 1, pp. 322ff. Learn about the grammatical-historical method of interpretation in Roy B. Zuck, *Basic Bible Interpretation* (Wheaton, Ill., Victor Books, 1991).

17. In connection with false doctrine, Ignatius says to the Magnesians, "As therefore the Lord did nothing without the Father . . . so neither do ye anything without the bishop." (*The Ante-Nicene Fathers,* vol. 1, p. 62.) One of

the most important treatises on the unique authority of the "successors of the Apostles" (bishops) to define doctrine is found in Irenaeus, "Against Heresies," *The Ante-Nicene Fathers,* vol. 1, pp. 414–417. In contrast to this focus on human authority, Justin Martyr said earlier that during Christian meetings, Bible reading from the New and Old Testaments was the main order of business along with the Eucharist. (Justin Martyr, "The First Apology of Justin," *The Ante-Nicene Fathers,* vol. 1, p. 186.)

18. Often this process was the result of pressure from the laity. However, the leadership of the church passively accepted the new forms of worship and, in any event, had failed to teach the truth in a way that would have provided an alternative. See Kenneth Scott LaTourette, *A History of Christianity,* vol. 1, pp. 208–212.

19. Both Luther and Calvin "believed that it was important for all Christians to read the Bible. They urged the state to help establish an educational system." (Merle L. Borrowman, "Education," *The Academic American Encyclopedia,* vol. 7, pp. 60–61.)

20. For instance, the church taught that the two swords found by Peter in Luke 22:38 stood for the two authorities established by God over human society. One sword was the civil government (based on the passage in Romans 13:4), and the other was the ecclesiastical (church) authority! On this basis, it became plausible for the church to use armed force against its enemies, as was done in the Crusades and in the many executions of dissenters in Europe over hundreds of years. (Geoffrey Bromiley, "The Interpretation of the Bible," Frank E. Gabelein, ed., *The Expositor's Bible Commentary* [Grand Rapids, Mich.: Zondervan, 1978], p. 69.)

21. See source materials relating to this power struggle in Brian Teirney, *The Crisis of Church and State: 1050–1300* (Englewood Cliffs, N.J.: Prentice-Hall, Inc., 1964). The

three-hundred-year history of the Inquisition can be studied in any survey of church or medieval history.

22. According to Gonzales, the persecution of Anabaptists, carried out by both Protestants and Catholics, involved more fatalities than the famous Roman persecution of Christians during the first two centuries of Christianity. Yet while everyone knows about the early persecution of Christians, this merciless persecution of the Anabaptists is virtually unknown to laymen today (Justo L. Gonzales, *The Story of Christianity,* vol. 2 [New York: Harper & Row, 1984], p. 56.).

23. Compare Deuteronomy 13:1-5; 2 Timothy 3:13. The peril of false prophecy has always been present, and it has always been the responsibility of the individual to discern it.

24. See also Hebrews 13:22, 24, where the author says, "Brothers, I urge you to bear with my word of exhortation. . . . Greet all your leaders and all God's people." We see the book is not addressed to leaders, but to the other members of the church. Also, Colossians 3:16 says, "Let the word of Christ dwell in you richly as you teach and admonish one another with all wisdom."

25. Compare Matthew 18:1-6; Luke 12:47-48; 2 Samuel 12:23. No doubt, the same applies to severely retarded or other mentally disabled people.

26. Many are documented in Don Richardson, *Eternity in Their Hearts* (Ventura, Calif.: Regal Books, 1981).

27. "Entrance into [nirvana] by any person means the dissolution at death of all the elements whose composition makes him the existent entity he now is." (E. A. Burtt, ed., *The Teachings of the Compassionate Buddha* [New York: The New American Library, 1955], p. 112.) So too in Taoism; verse 16 of the *Tao Te Ching* explains that to "touch ultimate emptiness . . . is to have stature. . . . Then though

you die, you shall not perish." (R. B. Blakney, trans., *The Way of Life: Lao Tzu* [New York: The New American Library, 1955], p. 68.)

28. See a clear neutral coverage of these religions in Denise L. Carmody and John T. Carmody, *Ways to the Center.*

TEN
Becoming Involved in Christianity

If you are seriously seeking, you will eventually reach a point where your questions have been substantially answered. Although you may still have doubts and unclear areas, you reach a point where no further progress is possible without action.

Suppose again you are in that three-hour party we started with in chapter 1. As you stand next to the closed door that supposedly offers healing, your new acquaintance tries to explain how you can know the door does lead to healing. He claims to have actually been on the other side of the door. He is able to give plausible explanations for why they have a cure for the disease killing everyone. Perhaps he also takes a polygraph as evidence that he is telling the truth. He produces photographs of the facilities beyond the door. He introduces you to others who have also been through the door.

This conversation could go on forever, and there would still be room for doubt. When would you reach the point where it would make sense to open the door and see for yourself if anything is there? Part of the answer to this question would depend on the amount of risk involved in opening the door. If there is little or no risk, you would be justified in opening the door fairly quickly. Perhaps this is where you are at this moment.

In Revelation 3:20, Jesus says, "Here I am! I stand at the door and knock. If anyone hears my voice and opens the door, I will come in and eat with him, and he with me." (Dining was considered the most personal kind of fellowship in this period.) Even those of us who have been involved in church and are members of churches still need to take Christ up on this offer if we have never done so before. This passage makes no mention of church membership. Instead, God is issuing a *personal* invitation to fellowship with him.

Will you open that door and let Christ enter your life right now? This is the best way to continue your investigation of Christianity. You may not understand everything, and you may have doubts or reservations. If you do have doubts, simply tell that to God and ask for confirmation that Christ has entered your life. You must admit that you fall short of God's standards, and that you are going to trust the death of Christ to pay for your sins so that God can forgive you.

Remember, when Christ says he will come in, he doesn't promise a sudden religious experience. He only promises to come in. Therefore, you may or may not have an immediate experience of his presence. People often experience a growing awareness of his presence as they begin to grow spiritually. Allow some time for the Spirit to manifest himself in your life.

BUILDING A RELATIONSHIP

Once you meet God personally, the next step is to get to know him. One of the most important things you can do, if you have prayed to God and opened the door of your life, is to find a Bible study group. Even if you haven't made the decision to receive Christ yet, finding a Bible study group might be one of the best ways to move toward a decision.

Considering how many extremist groups are around today under the name "Christian," the choice of a Christian fellowship needs to be made with some care. In this book, we have consistently stressed that only biblical Christianity commends itself. The Bible has both reliable answers and built-in credibility. But a group based primarily on tradition lacks this credibility and is insufficient by itself. A new Christian needs help getting started in Bible study, and this should be available in many Bible study groups.

Since some groups have little to do with biblical Christianity, you should make every effort to distinguish between churches or groups that are faithful to the message of the Bible and those that are not. For instance, any church that is not involved in regular Bible study is not trustworthy. This should be obvious. Why wouldn't a church based on the Bible study the Bible? The fact is that some modern church leaders have forsaken belief in the Bible and are actually embarrassed by the supernatural. Others see the Bible as no more enlightening than other holy books. Such leaders cannot help you understand the true God of the Bible.

Many authoritarian groups in operation today call for unconditional obedience to church authority. This kind of group should be carefully avoided because it is elevating human authority to the same level as the Bible. Such a group may resent questioning of its teachings. Therefore, a church or study group that will not at least try to answer your questions is also not trustworthy.[1] It is also wise to avoid groups that are highly legalistic, bossy, or restrictive.

Jesus said the fruit of teachers or prophets would show whether or not they should be trusted. Foremost among these fruits is a real caring love (Galatians 5:22; John 13:34). Look for a caring group of Christians who can help you in your study of the Bible.

For growing Christians, the Bible is like food. As with physical food, any young Christian who doesn't eat may be alive, but will be malnourished. Peter said: "Like newborn babes, long for the pure milk of the word, that by it you may grow in respect to salvation" (1 Peter 2:2, NASB).

Jesus also taught that the Bible is essential for growth: "If you abide in My word, then you are truly disciples of Mine; and you shall know the truth, and the truth shall make you free" (John 8:31-3, NASB).

If you have doubts, the Bible will also help you deal with them. As we understand the answers given in Scripture, our faith is strengthened. "Faith comes from hearing the message, and the message is heard through the word of Christ" (Romans 10:17).

On the basis of these passages alone, it should be clear that any group that puts down the Bible or discourages you from studying it is behaving suspiciously. On the other hand, if you find a group of sincere Christians engaged in learning and living the truths of the Bible, you are in a position where God will be able to give you more insight through the agency of other Christians.

One of the easiest and most reliable ways to find a good Bible study group in most American and European cities is to contact a parachurch organization. Navigators, Inter-Varsity Christian Fellowship, Youth for Christ, and Campus Crusade for Christ are examples of student-oriented parachurch groups based in most metropolitan areas. Ask one of these groups where a good church or Bible study group is in your area. They will know which churches and fellowships are faithful to Scripture.

It is a good idea to find a Christian bookstore in your city. There you will find a wide range of books featuring Christian thinking on biblical themes.

Prayer: Direct communication. A relationship cannot go far without personal communication. Prayer is another element needed in spiritual growth. When praying, you can address God as Lord and friend (Matthew 6:7-8; John 15:14-15). There is no exact thing you need to say. Simply speak to God about the things you are going through and the way you feel. You can share with God anything bothering you (Philippians 4:6-7).

Finally, you need never fear that you will offend God and cause him to withdraw from you. Romans 8:1 says: "Therefore, there is now no condemnation for those who are in Christ Jesus," and in John 6:37 Jesus said: "Whoever comes to me I will never drive away."

These passages and others show that you are secure in your relationship with God even if you sin. Like a loving father who may be distressed if his children do wrong, God may be grieved at times, but he will not withdraw, as long as you have trusted that Christ's death forgives your sin. His patience is infinite.

As you grow spiritually, you will begin to notice evidences of the presence of the Holy Spirit in your life, including a new outlook on life and a growing hunger for the Bible and Christian fellowship. Your own relationship with God will become more rewarding and tangible. Many Christians find they have a new sensitivity to right and wrong. Christians often find themselves becoming uncomfortable with some activities they used to be able to do with no problem. And usually, Christians discover a growing desire to see others meet Christ.

God will reassure you in various ways if you place yourself in a position to receive blessings from him. As spiritual growth continues, you will eventually reach the place where you are as sure of Christ's presence with you as you are of the presence of your other friends.

NOTES

1. Remember that if you have probing questions, some Christians may think you are attacking their faith. To avoid misunderstanding, try to be as polite as possible in raising questions.